Fun with
SUNBONNET SUE

Terrece Beesley and Trice Boerens

Martingale
& COMPANY
Bothell, Washington

Credits

Artist..Terrece Beesley
Artist..Trice Boerens
Designer ....Cherie Hanson
Editor ....Margaret Shields Marti

Fun with Sunbonnet Sue
© 1999 by Terrece Beesley and Trice Boerens

Library of Congress Cataloging-in-Publication Data

Boerens , Trice
Fun with Sunbonnet Sue / Trice Boerens , Terrece Beesley.
p.   cm.
ISBN 1-56477-268-3
1. Applique—Patterns.   2. Quilts.   I. Beesley , Terrece.
II. Title.
TT779.B64   1999
746 . 44'5—dc21   99 - 10299
                                      CIP

Printed in Hong Kong

04 03 02 01 00 99   6 5 4 3 2 1

Martingale
& C O M P A N Y

Martingale & Company
PO Box 118
Bothell, WA 98041-0118 USA
www.patchwork.com

MISSION STATEMENT

WE ARE DEDICATED TO PROVIDING QUALITY PRODUCTS
AND SERVICE BY WORKING TOGETHER TO INSPIRE
CREATIVITY AND TO ENRICH THE LIVES WE TOUCH.

TABLE OF CONTENTS

INTRODUCTION

It's just a guess on our part, but we can imagine that already you are picturing half a dozen ways to enjoy Sunbonnet Sue and her friend Overall Bill in your world. A quilt for a child's room? Something to brighten the corner of the sun porch? A pillow for a new nephew?

Sunbonnet Sue and Overall Bill are about as traditional as quilting can get, and then again, they are not. As familiar as they are, these charming figures take on new personalities with each quilter who works on them.

The pieces presented in this book can be worked in either needle-turn appliqué or fused appliqué. Needle-turn appliqué is the kind of handwork your grandmother had in her lap on long summer afternoons. Her rhythmical, even stitches made it seem almost as though the design piece were being woven into the background. Fused appliqué is the contemporary technique your best friend used to decorate the tote she made you. Quite simply, paper-backed fusible web and a hot iron allow you to join two pieces of fabric without making a single stitch. Pretty easy!

Certainly both techniques have their place in the world of today's needleworker. In either case, you bring these charming characters to life through your fabric choices. Guessing again, we think you have a closet filled with pretty fabrics that you think aren't big enough for much, but that will be perfect for Bill's overalls or Sue's cat. This is the opportunity you've known would come your way. Match up your fabrics in coordinating sets of two or three, and you'll be ready to start a project!

Now dig through your embroidery floss and button box. And stop by the quilt store. All the little things that have caught your fancy in the past can find a home in one of the designs on these pages. We called a halt to the embellishments on some of these designs so we could get this book to you, but you have all the time in the world to be creative. Go ahead–start, but don't stop until you've tried all those ideas you've been saving. You'll love having Bill and Sue come to life through your fingers. We did!

Terrece Beesley and Trice Boerens

5

BASIC INSTRUCTIONS

Appliqué should have smooth curves and sharp points. Practice and patience have long been recommended as the best tools. One of the pleasures of appliqué is working with the small fabric pieces, turning them one way or another to achieve a new effect. Even the most difficult pieces can be worked with a needle-turn method. Contemporary needleworkers have the option of using fused appliqué, a technique which employs paper-backed fusible webbing. Both techniques are used in the projects in this book.

Preparing Your Project

Tightly woven, 100% cotton fabric is your best choice for quiltmaking. Yardages are based upon 44"-wide fabrics with trimmed selvages, and they allow for shrinkage and differences in layout. Wash, dry, and press all fabrics before marking and cutting any pieces. All cutting measurements for pieced segments include ¼" seam allowances. Appliqué patterns do not include seam allowances; you will need to add those as you cut out the pieces. When the instructions call for scraps, usually the pieces are smaller than a piece of typing paper. For anything larger, the instructions specify an amount.

Work with good scissors. Small, sharp scissors that cut to the point are a good choice both for cutting out the small design pieces and for clipping. Rotary cutters are a wonderful aid for cutting blocks, strips, and bias binding.

Turn your imagination loose—the sky doesn't always have to be blue. When choosing fabric, don't limit yourself to solids and small-scale prints. A large-scale print might include just the splash of color you need for a tiny appliqué piece. If you have found the right shade but the print is too busy, consider using the "wrong" side. (Who's to say what's wrong and what's right in a quilt?)

First select the clothing for Sue and Bill—small-scale plaids, checks, stripes, and prints work well. Then select the fabrics for the other pieces of the design. Use fabrics that are tightly woven, especially for small pieces, because they will fray if the weave is loose and be more difficult to work with. Follow the color key included with the patterns only to the extent that you like our combinations and have scraps that are similar. Branch out whenever you can.

Finish a few blocks or the pillow top before you buy fabric for sashing, borders, or ruffles. The fabric you select for finishing the project should complement but not overpower or compete with the blocks. Take the blocks with you and try them against several fabric choices.

You may wish to match the grain line of the appliqué pieces to the grain line of the block, but allow for the interesting effect of cutting a piece that's somewhere between the bias and the grain line. Besides, Sue's skirt does not always hang with the grain line. When pieces overlap, such as the sleeve of Bill's shirt and his overalls, select fabrics that contrast.

Needle-Turn Appliqué

Traditional appliqué is needle-turn appliqué, and the needle is the most important tool. Choose a long, fine needle, preferably a #11 or #12 Sharp, that feels good to you. Work with short lengths of fine cotton thread, and sew with one strand. If you can't match the color of the fabric exactly, a shade that's darker and duller will blend better than lighter and brighter. For a medium-value print with several colors, a medium gray will blend well.

Needle-turn appliqué is simply turning under the seam allowance on a design piece and slipstitching it to the background fabric. Pin or baste the design pieces in place. You may wish to trace the patterns onto the background, using an air-soluble or water-soluble marker, to assure correct positioning. As you plan the placement, note which pieces overlap others. For example, the top of Sue's shoes always tuck under her dress.

Use your needle to turn under the seam allowance 1" or 2" ahead of where you are stitching, creasing the fold line with your fingers. Slipstitch the appliqué to the background fabric, using tiny, even stitches about ⅛" apart on straight edges and even closer around inside curves and sharp points.

To make the edge lie flat on inside curves, clip the seam allowance almost to the fold line. Clip excess fabric from tips of corners to eliminate bulk. Inverted points, or cleavages, such as the top, inside point of a heart, call for special attention because they are subject to fraying. To prevent fraying, take smaller stitches as you near a cleavage, and make several overcast stitches at the point itself.

Fused Appliqué

Each of the designs in this book may be prepared as fused appliqué. A little experimentation, and you will be ready to try your hand at this easy way to bring Sunbonnet Sue and Overall Bill to life!

Begin by acquainting yourself with the properties of paper-backed fusible web. On the smooth side—the paper side—you can trace patterns using an ordinary pencil. On the rough side you can feel the crystals that melt when they come in contact with the heat of an iron.

All the patterns in this book face the right way; that is, the way they appear in the finished project. For fused appliqué you need to transfer the patterns to the fusible web in reverse, as outlined in the following instructions, so that they will face the right way after fusing.

Preparing the Pattern Pieces

First, trace the entire pattern onto tracing paper, using a heavy pencil line. You will use this pattern twice—first to trace the pieces, and later as an overlay to guide you when fusing. Turn the tracing-paper pattern face down. Place the fusible web, paper side up, over the pattern. Place both pieces over a light box or hold them up to a window, then retrace the pattern onto the paper side of the fusible web. Trace pieces that are to be cut from the same fabric (such as all green leaves) in groups, allowing about ¼" between pieces. (The colors on the pattern pieces indicate which pieces to cut from the same fabric.) Cut the web in one piece, about ½" from the pencil lines. You are ready to fuse a piece or group of pieces to fabric.

Know your iron. A few experiments and you can tell how many seconds and what temperature setting gives you the best results. It doesn't take very much long to fuse the web to the fabric, maybe 2 or 3 seconds. Fusing is like preparing pasta; you don't want to overcook it.

Place the rough side of the web against the wrong side of the fabric (if it has a wrong side). Iron for 2 or 3 seconds until your pattern piece is fused to the fabric. At this point, your pattern piece is still backwards from the photo and from the pattern in the book (Diagram 1).

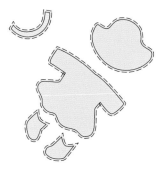

Diagram 1

Preparing the Templates

Another key to success is using templates. The template is simply tissue paper with a shape from the pattern traced, then cut out. It's used to help frame the space as you begin to appliqué the pieces in the design. The template works with the pattern overlay to guide you in placing the pattern pieces.

Pinning the Layers Together

Place the template over the background fabric, pinning the corners (Diagram 2). Then place the pattern overlay right side up over the template and background fabric, aligning the template and the pattern so they match (Diagram 3). Pin the pattern overlay along the top edge only. The pattern overlay will remain in the same place throughout the appliqué process, but the template is temporary.

Diagram 2

Diagram 3

Fusing the Pieces

Cut out the pattern pieces along the pencil lines. When working with small pieces, it's best to cut only two or three at a time. Peel the paper backing from the web. Place the cut-out fabric piece right side up on the background, using the template and the pattern overlay as your guide (Diagram 4). Now the piece will correspond with the photo and the pattern. Fuse in place.

Diagram 4

Continue to fuse a few pieces at a time, following the pattern overlay (Diagram 5). When the area outlined by the template has been completed, remove the template and throw it away. Continue to fuse pieces until the pattern is complete. When they have cooled, check to see that all the pieces are adhering well, especially at the edges.

Diagram 5

- When working with solid colors, you may turn the web in any direction you want. In fact, variety in the grain positioning enhances the finished product. If the fabric pattern is important to the design, such as stripes in a border piece, plan carefully as you trace the pieces onto the web and fuse the web onto the fabric.

- In most cases when the instructions call for a print, the appliqué piece is small and does not contrast much with the background color; for example, the fabric may have small white leaves against a cream background. In some cases, the designated fabric color is uneven and when the small pieces are cut out, they appear to be from different fabrics. The variations add to the interest of the design.

- When the embroidered design on a project contains lettering or is more detailed than you wish to draw freehand, use a water-soluble or air-soluble marking pen or transfer pencil. For any of the tools, follow the manufacturer's instructions and experiment before using it on a project. To use the transfer pencil, trace the lettering from the pattern in the book onto tracing paper, using a heavy pencil line. Then turn the pattern over. Trace the lettering using the transfer pencil; it will be backwards. Place the transfer pencil pattern right side up where you want it on the fabric. Iron.

Constructing the Quilt

To prepare two pieces for joining, place them right sides together, matching seams when appropriate, and securing them with pins. Stitch with a ¼" seam, using about 12 stitches per inch. For best results, press seams as you go. Always press a seam before crossing it with another.

The instructions usually call for the appliqué designs to be worked on one block at a time so you won't have to contend with the bulk of the whole quilt top. Some pieces of the design are placed on the edges and sewn into the seams as the blocks are joined to sashing or to each other. The rows are sewn to more sashing, or to each other, and then together to form the quilt top. The border frames the design and adds some stability.

Mitering the Corners

The diagonal lines of mitered corners add a crisp finish to borders and require only a little extra effort. To ensure perfect mitered corners, begin by folding each border strip widthwise to find its center. Mark the center with a pin.

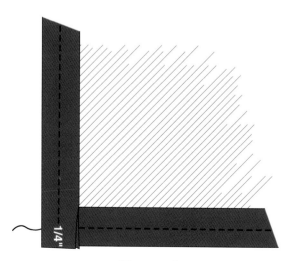

Diagram 6

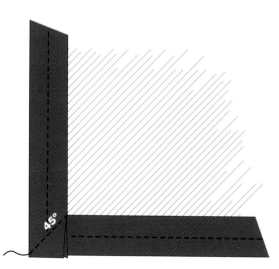

Diagram 7

Also mark the center of each edge of the quilt top. With right sides together, match the center of the border to the center of the quilt top. Stitch the pieces together, starting and stopping ¼" from the corners; backstitch (Diagram 6). Repeat the centering and stitching for each edge, allowing the border strips to hang loose.

Fold the right sides of two adjacent strips together and stitch a diagonal (45-degree) seam (Diagram 7). Open the border pieces to check your work. The diagonal seam and the two seams joining the borders to the quilt top should all meet but not overlap. Trim the seam allowance on the diagonal seam to ¼". Repeat for each corner.

Quilting the Quilt
Quilting stitches are used to secure the backing, batting, and quilt top together, often in a pattern that enhances the design. Quilting can be done either by hand or machine and with thread that matches or contrasts.

Mark the quilting lines on the quilt top. If you want to quilt parallel to seams, you don't need to mark those lines. Place the backing fabric on a large, flat surface with the batting centered over it. Then layer the quilt top over both. Baste the three layers together, working from the center out. In most cases, it is best to quilt with quilting thread.

Binding the Quilt
Binding covers the remaining raw edges and serves as a nice finishing touch that adds to the life of the quilt. To make binding strips, cut bias strips in segments as long as possible. Then join the ends with ¼" seams. Fold the binding in half lengthwise and press. Place the binding on the quilt top with right sides together and raw edges matching. Stitch the binding to the quilt top, rounding the corners or mitering them. Fold the bias to the back and slipstitch it in place, covering the stitching line.

To miter the binding, stitch the binding to the quilt top, starting and stopping ¼" from the corners; backstitch (Diagram 8). Fold the bias at a right angle, placing the fold on the edge of the quilt (Diagram 9). Resume stitching with a backstitch ¼" from the corner. Repeat at each corner. Fold the binding at a diagonal and slipstitch it to the back of the quilt.

Finishing Touch
Always sign and date your work. You may use a permanent pen or embroider your name and the date. Some quilters sign and date their work on a separate piece of fabric and slipstitch it to the back; others write or embroider on the quilt back itself. With either method, the information enriches the quilt.

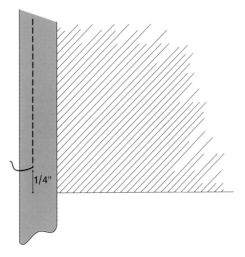

1/4"

Diagram 8

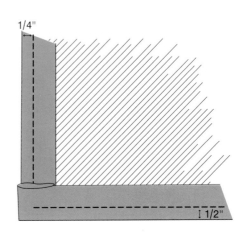

1/4"

1 1/2"

Diagram 9

Embroidery Stitches

Backstitch

Bring the needle up at 1, down at 2, up at 3. Go back down at 1, and continue in this manner.

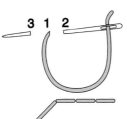

Cross Stitch

Each single cross is made of two stitches forming a cross. Large areas or rows may be worked by first stitching across the row from left to right. Complete the crosses by working back across the row from right to left. All top stitches should slant in the same direction.

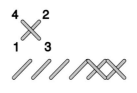

Buttonhole Stitch

This stitch is worked from left to right. Bring the thread out at 1. Insert the needle at 2, and bring it out at 3, stitching over the first stitch. Insert the needle at 4 and repeat.

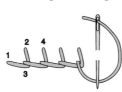

Chain Stitch

Bring the needle up at 1, hold down a small loop of thread, and insert the needle at 2. Bring the needle up at 3 and insert it at 4, guiding the needle over the loop and securing the previous loop with the loop just formed. Repeat, securing each loop with the next to form a chain. Take a small stitch over the end of the last loop to secure the end.

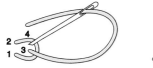

Couching

Use these simple stitches to anchor a length of floss or ribbon to fabric.

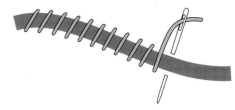

French Knot

Bring the needle up at 1 and wrap floss once (or twice) around the shaft of the needle. Insert the needle into the fabric at 2. Change the size of your knot by varying the strands used or wrapping more times.

Satin Stitch

Bring the needle up at 1 and down at 2, making parallel stitches. Repeat to fill a desired area.

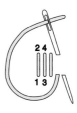

Spider Stitch

Begin by laying five straight stitches, radiating evenly from the center. Darn thread under and over the spokes formed by the straight stitches. (Stitches should lie close together, not loose as in diagram).

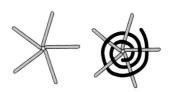

Stem Stitch

Bring the needle up at 1, down at 2, up at 3, and down at 4, keeping the thread to the left of the needle.

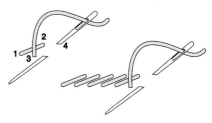

SUNBONNET SUE
HEART PILLOW

Materials

1 yard of 44"-wide mauve print for wide
   ruffle and pillow back
¾ yard of 44"-wide rose fabric for
   pillow front and narrow ruffle
13" x 13" piece of light blue print for
   large heart
Scraps of cotton fabric in these colors:
   pink, pink check, pink floral print,
   lavender, purple, purple print,
   turquoise, and cream
Thread to match fabrics
Embroidery floss in these colors: light
   pink and brown
16" pillow form
Tracing paper
Dressmaker's chalk
Water-soluble marking pen

Appliqué the Design

Note: Refer to "Needle-Turn Appliqué" on page 6 for general instructions. Refer to the project photo and pattern for placement.

1. Trace the patterns individually onto tracing paper and cut apart. Referring to the photo and the color key, pin the pattern pieces to the desired fabric and cut out, adding a ¼" seam allowance to all edges. Note that the heart pattern is in 3 pieces; join to make one large heart pattern. Cut 2 flowers and 4 leaves.

2. From the rose fabric, cut a 16" x 16" piece for the pillow top. Center the heart over the pillow top and pin in place. Appliqué the heart.

3. Appliqué Sue's shoes, the ruffle, and dress.

4. Appliqué the turquoise heart, then the hand and the bow on her dress.

5. Appliqué Sue's arm and the hat.

6. Appliqué a leaf in each corner. Appliqué a flower over the leaves in the 2 bottom corners.

Embroider the Details

Note: For the embroidery stitches, follow the instructions on page 11. Refer to the photo and pattern for placement.

1. Mark the embroidery lines on the bow and hat with a water-soluble pen.

2. Using 2 strands of light pink floss, buttonhole-stitch around the edges of the hat and both flowers. Cross-stitch the hat band. Sew French knots on the turquoise heart.

3. Using 2 strands of brown floss, buttonhole-stitch around both shoes. Stem-stitch the details in the bow.

Make the Pillow

1. From the mauve fabric, cut a 16" x 16" piece for the back of the pillow. Also cut 5"-wide bias strips, piecing as needed, to equal at least 2½ yards.

2. From the rose fabric, cut 3½"-wide bias strips, piecing as needed, to equal at least 2½ yards.

3. Join the ends of the narrow bias strip to make a continuous piece. Fold the bias strip in half lengthwise and press. Sew gathering threads along the long raw edge. Fold the bias strip into quarters and mark the quarters with pins. Place the pins at each corner of the pillow front. Gather the bias strip to fit the edges of the pillow front; pin in place. Fold the ruffle toward the center, out of the way, and stitch the narrow ruffle to the pillow front with a ¼" seam.

4. Repeat Step 3 with the wide ruffle.

5. Stitch the pillow front and pillow back right sides together, using a ¼" seam and leaving an opening on one edge. Turn the cover right side out; insert the pillow form. Slipstitch the opening closed.

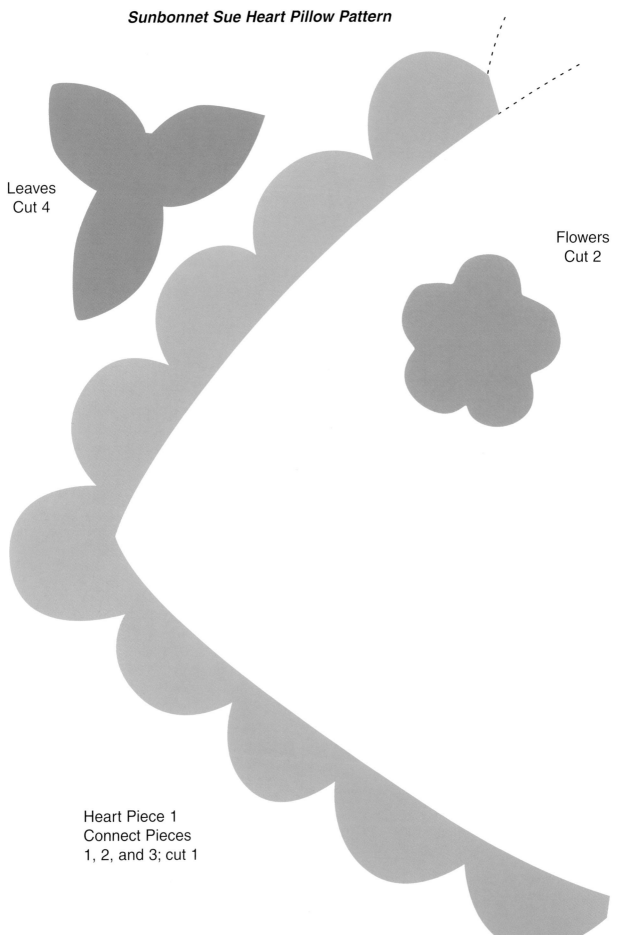

Leaves
Cut 4

Flowers
Cut 2

Heart Piece 1
Connect Pieces
1, 2, and 3; cut 1

Heart Piece 2

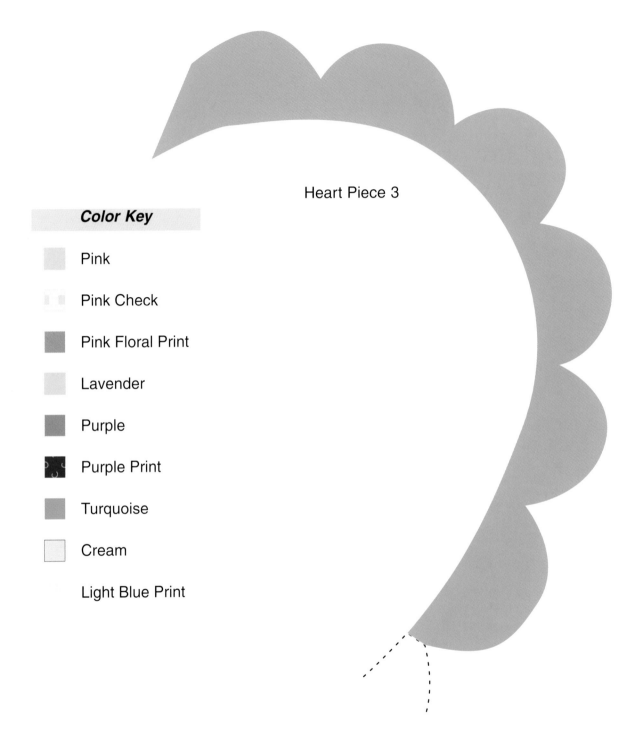

Heart Piece 3

Color Key

Pink

Pink Check

Pink Floral Print

Lavender

Purple

Purple Print

Turquoise

Cream

Light Blue Print

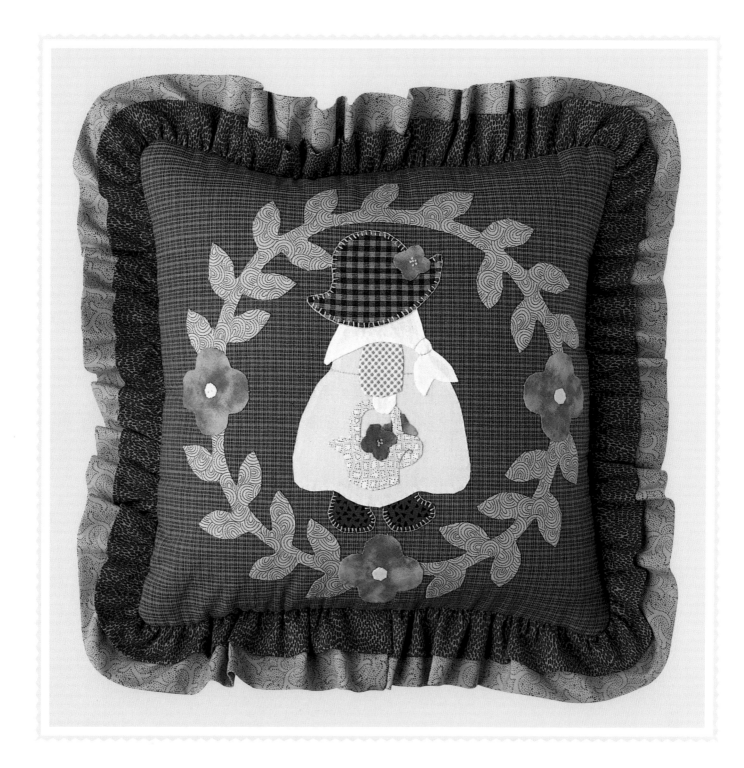

SUNBONNET SUE
Wreath Pillow

Materials

1 yard of 44"-wide light blue print for wide ruffle and pillow back

½ yard of 44"-wide dark blue print for narrow ruffle

¼ yard of light blue print for appliqué wreath

16" x 16" piece of medium blue plaid fabric for pillow front

Scraps of cotton fabric in these colors: white, very light blue, navy blue check, turquoise, blue/cream check, tan print, and blue/black print

Thread to match fabrics

Embroidery floss in these colors: tan and light blue

16" pillow form

Tracing paper

Dressmaker's chalk

Water-soluble marking pen

Appliqué the Design

Note: Refer to "Needle-Turn Appliqué" on page 6 for general instructions. Refer to the project photo and pattern for placement.

1. Trace the patterns individually onto tracing paper and cut apart. Referring to the photo and the color key, pin the pattern pieces to the desired fabric and cut out, adding a ¼" seam allowance to all edges. Note that the pattern for the top of the wreath is in 2 pieces; join to make one. Cut 3 large turquoise flowers and 3 small turquoise flowers.

2. Fold the pillow top into quarters and mark the center. Use chalk to mark a 10"-wide circle on the center of the pillow top.

3. Pin the wreath pieces over the chalk line, allowing for the large turquoise flowers. Appliqué the wreath pieces (Diagram 1). Appliqué the large turquoise flowers, then the flower centers.

4. Appliqué Sue's shoes, then the dress.

5. Appliqué a small turquoise flower behind the basket, then the basket and the second small flower. Appliqué Sue's hand, then the sleeve.

6. Appliqué scarf, then the hat (Diagram 2).

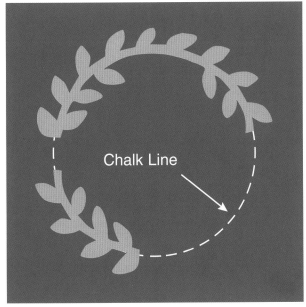

Chalk Line

Diagram 1

Diagram 2

Embroider the Details

Note: For the embroidery stitches, follow the instructions on page 11. Refer to the photo and pattern for placement.

1. Mark the embroidery lines for the curve in the basket, the waist of the dress, and the knot in the tie with a water-soluble pen; see the photo on page 18.

2. Using 1 strand of tan floss, stem-stitch the curve in the basket, the waist of the dress, and the knot in the tie. Using 2 strands of tan floss, buttonhole-stitch around the hat.

3. Appliqué the third small flower. Using 2 strands of tan floss, make a cluster of French knots in the second and third small flowers.

4. Using 2 strands of light blue floss, buttonhole-stitch around the shoes.

Make the Pillow

1. From the light blue print, cut a 16" x 16" piece for the back of the pillow. Also cut 5"-wide bias strips, piecing as needed, to equal at least 2½ yards.

2. From the dark blue print, cut 3½"-wide bias strips, piecing as needed, to equal at least 2½ yards.

3. Join the ends of the narrow bias strip to make a continuous piece. Fold the bias strip in half lengthwise and press. Sew gathering threads along the long raw edge. Fold the bias strip into quarters and mark the quarters with pins. Place the pins at each corner of the pillow front. Gather the bias strip to fit the edges of the pillow front; pin in place. Fold the ruffle toward the center, out of the way, and stitch the narrow ruffle to the pillow front with a scant ¼" seam.

4. Repeat Step 3 with the wide ruffle.

5. Stitch the pillow front and pillow back right sides together, using a ¼" seam and leaving an opening on one edge. Turn the cover right side out; insert the pillow form. Slipstitch the opening closed.

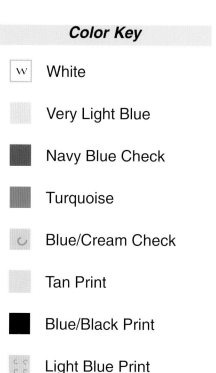

Color Key

w — White

Very Light Blue

Navy Blue Check

Turquoise

Blue/Cream Check

Tan Print

Blue/Black Print

Light Blue Print

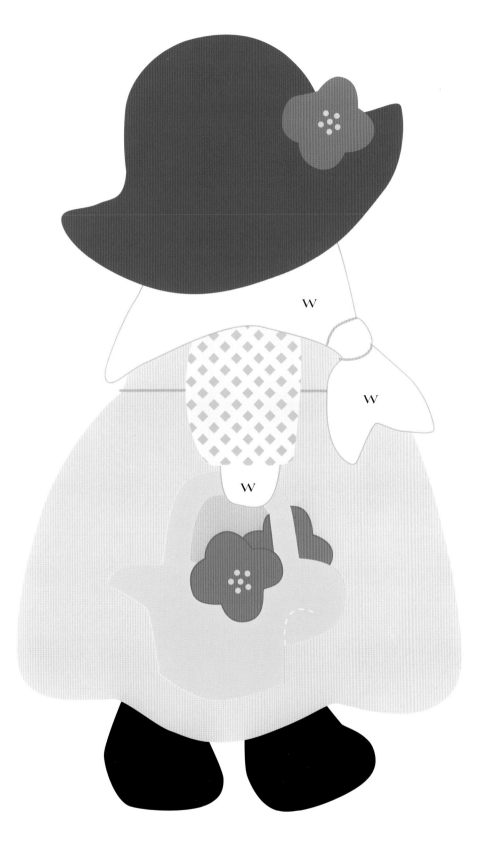

Sunbonnet Sue Wreath Pillow Pattern

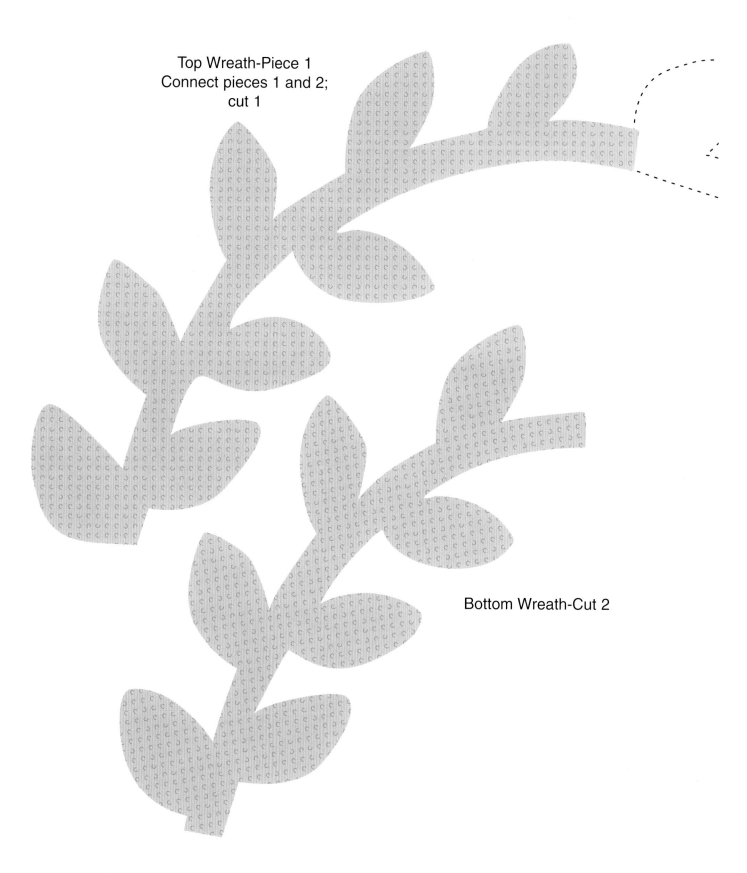

Top Wreath-Piece 1
Connect pieces 1 and 2;
cut 1

Bottom Wreath-Cut 2

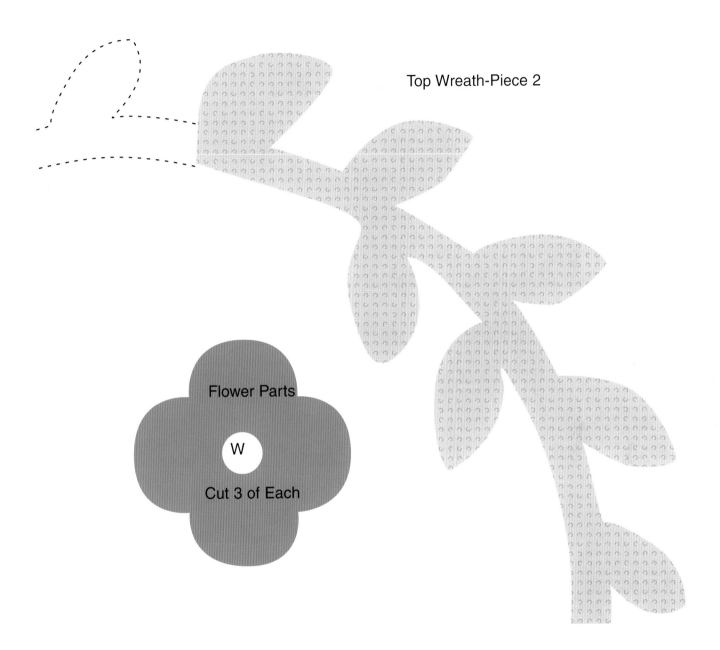

Top Wreath-Piece 2

Flower Parts

W

Cut 3 of Each

"WELCOME"
Door Topper

Materials

1 yard of 44"-wide navy blue print fabric for binding

1 yard of 44"-wide blue print fabric for background and backing

½ yard of 44"-wide rose fabric for border and apples

¼ yard of 44" wide blue/black print fabric for band at base

10" x 13" piece of brown fabric for background

Scraps of cotton fabric in these colors: brown print, dark green, olive, gold print, blue chambray, white, blue print, black, tan print, turquoise, yellow, green print, red plaid print, and rust

Thread to match fabrics

Embroidery floss in these colors: gold, yellow-green, bright yellow, turquoise, blue, brown, and black

White quilting thread

½ yard batting

Tracing paper and pencil

Dressmaker's chalk

Air-soluble marking pen

Prepare the Background

1. Referring to Diagram 1 on page 26, enlarge the pattern onto a piece of tracing paper. You may need to tape together pieces of tracing paper to make a piece large enough. Cut out the pattern around the outside edges. Cut away the brown sections of the pattern, creating a window in the paper pattern.

2. Pin the pattern to the blue print fabric, and use chalk to trace around the pattern and around the inside of the window. Cut the 1"-wide arched border off the paper pattern and set aside. Reposition the pattern on the fabric, and use the chalk to trace the new line of the arch. Cut out the blue background on the outside pattern lines. Cut away the inside of the window, cutting ¼" inside the chalk line.

3. Center the brown fabric behind the window. Fold under the ¼" seam allowance and slipstitch the blue print to the brown fabric, clipping the seam as needed along the arched edge.

4. Pin the 1"-wide border pattern to the rose fabric. Cut 1 piece, adding a ¼" seam allowance to the inside edge. Pin the border to the background. Fold under the seam allowance, and slipstitch the inside edge along the chalk line, clipping the seam allowance as needed to make the arch.

Appliqué the Design

Note: Refer to "Needle-Turn Appliqué" on page 6 for general instructions. Refer to the project photo and pattern for placement.

1. Trace the patterns individually onto tracing paper and cut apart. Referring to the photo and the color key, pin the pattern pieces to the desired fabrics and cut out, adding a ¼" seam allowance to all edges.

2. Mark the vertical center of the background. Appliqué the letters for "Welcome" to the background, placing the *C* on the vertical center. The outside base corners of the *W* and *E* are 1" from the corner of the brown window.

3. Appliqué the fabric pieces for Bill in this order: shoes, shirt collar, overalls, cuffs, hand, sleeve, and hat.

4. Repeat for Sue, beginning with the shoes, then the dress, apron, hand, sleeve, and hat.

5. Cut out the fabric pieces for the pie and appliqué in this order: pie pan, pie crust, and apple.

6. Appliqué the tree trunk to the left of the window, placing it parallel to and 1½" from the edge of the window. Then appliqué the grass and apples.

7. Appliqué the stool, then the dog to the right of the window.

Embroider the Details

Note: For the embroidery stitches, follow the instructions on page 11. Refer to the photo and pattern for placement.

1. Mark the embroidery lines on the pie crust and dog with a water-soluble pen.

2. Using 2 strands of gold floss, buttonhole-stitch around all apples. Sew running stitches on the tree trunk, stitching just inside and parallel to the edge of the fabric. Repeat for the grass, pie pan, dress, and apron. Tack stitch around all letters.

3. Using 2 strands of black floss, buttonhole-stitch the edges of both hats. Satin-stitch the dog's nose, backstitch its mouth and ear, and make French knots for its eyes. Sew running stitches to outline the dog's legs. Tack-stitch the outside edge of the dog.

4. Satin-stitch leaves on or near the apples, using 2 strands of yellow-green floss. Couch the stem of the apple atop the pie.

5. Using 2 strands of brown floss,buttonhole-stitch around the pie crust. Stem-stitch the details on the pie.

6. Using 2 strands of bright yellow floss, buttonhole-stitch around Bill's sleeve.

7. Using 2 strands of turquoise floss, buttonhole-stitch around Sue's sleeve and Bill's overalls.

8. Tack-stitch the outside edges of Bill's and Sue's shoes and the stool, using 2 strands of blue floss. Sew running stitches inside Bill's cuffs.

Diagram 1

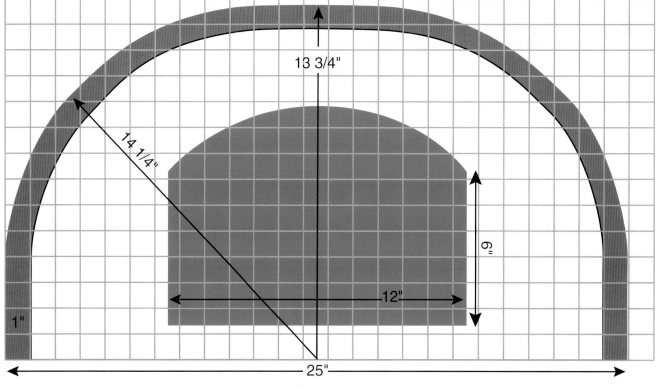

13 3/4"

14 1/4"

9"

12"

1"

25"

Each Square Equals 1"

Complete the Door Topper

1. Cut a piece of blue/black fabric 3¾" x 25" for the base. Sew it to the bottom edge of the design piece. Using chalk, mark lines at a 45-degree angle 1" apart across the base.

2. Layer the batting over the wrong side of the blue backing. Center the front over the layered pieces and baste all layers together.

3. Using white thread, quilt around the outside edges of both figures and the pie, including the outline of the shoes. Quilt inside the window. Also quilt around each letter, the tree section, and the dog section. Quilt inside the rose border and above the base on the blue background. Quilt the diagonal lines in the base.

4. Trim the batting and back to match the outside edges of the design piece. From the navy print, cut 2½"-wide bias strips, piecing together as needed to equal at least 78". Fold the bias in half lengthwise; press. Fold up ½" at the end of the binding. Starting along the bottom edge, stitch the binding to the right side of the wall hanging ½" from the edge. Stop ½" from the corner; backstitch. Fold the bias at the corner at a right angle. Resume stitching along the arch, stopping ½" from the corner. Miter the corner as before, then finish stitching. Overlap the binding ½" at the ends and trim excess.

5. Fold the bias to the back and slipstitch, covering the stitching line and mitering each corner.

Color Key

Brown

Brown Print

Dark Green

Olive

Gold Print

Blue Chambray

White

Blue Print

Black

Tan Print

Turquoise

Yellow

Green Print

Red Plaid Print

Rust

Rose

W

W

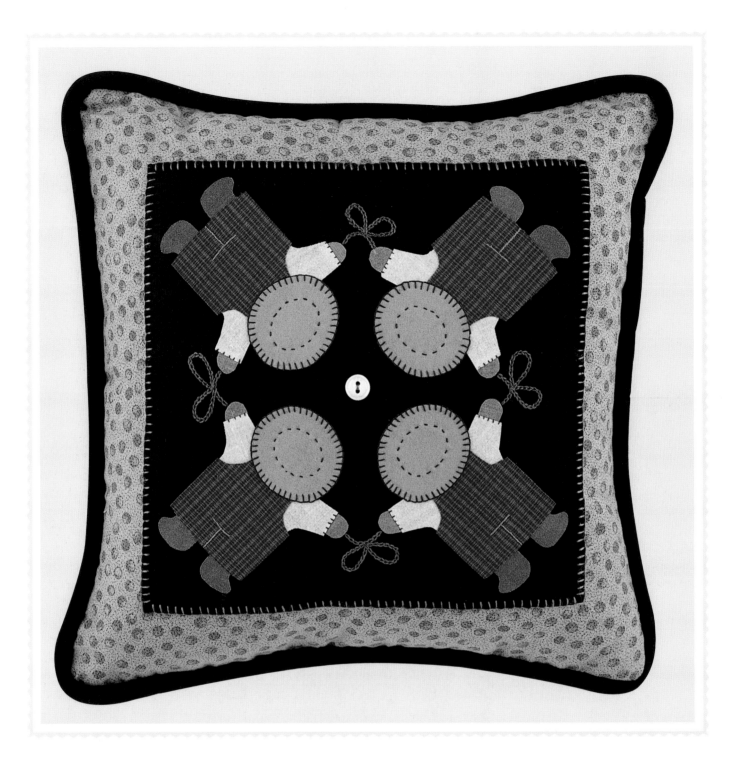

BILL-IN-A-CORNER
Pillow

Materials

½ yard of 44"-wide tan print fabric for pillow

⅜ yard of 44"-wide black fabric for piping

Scraps of cotton fabric in these colors: light brown, white, blue plaid, tan, and purple

10" x 10" piece of black felt

Thread to match fabrics

Embroidery floss in these colors: brown, blue, and green

2 yards of ½"-wide cording

14" pillow form

½"-diameter white button

Tracing paper for patterns

Dressmaker's chalk

Water-soluble marking pen

Appliqué the Design

Note: Refer to "Needle-Turn Appliqué" on page 6 for general instructions. Refer to the project photo and pattern for placement.

1. Trace the patterns individually onto tracing paper and cut apart. Referring to the photo and the color key, pin the pattern pieces to the desired fabric and cut out, adding a ¼" seam allowance to all edges.

2. Fold the black felt into quarters and mark the center. Appliqué the fabric pieces for Bill in the corner of the felt square in this order: feet, hands, sleeves, overalls, and hat. Repeat at the remaining corners to complete 4 Bill figures.

Embroider the Details

Note: For the embroidery stitches, follow the instructions on page 11. Refer to the photo and pattern for placement.

1. Mark the embroidery lines with a water-soluble pen.

2. Using 2 strands of brown floss, sew running stitches in the crown of the hats. Buttonhole-stitch around each hat. Tack-stitch each sleeve.

3. Using 2 strands of green floss, chain-stitch the bows between the figures.

4. Using 2 strands of blue floss, backstitch the line between the legs and sew a button in the center of the design.

Finish the Pillow

1. From the tan print fabric, cut two 14" x 14" pieces.

2. Trim the black felt to 9¼" x 9¼" with the design centered. Center the black felt square on the right side of one tan print piece. Pin in place and buttonhole-stitch all edges using 2 strands of blue floss.

3. From the black fabric, cut 1½"-wide bias strips, piecing as needed, to equal at least 2 yards. To make piping, place the cording in the center of the wrong side of the bias strip. Fold the bias strip over the cording and stitch close to the cording using a zipper foot. Trim seam allowance ¼" from the stitching line. Place the piping on the right side of the pillow front. Begin stitching 1" from end of piping. Stitch with a ¼" seam, rounding corners and clipping the seam allowance as needed. At the end, trim the piping to overlap by 1". Remove the stitching from one end for about 1"; trim the cording so the ends just meet. Fold over the raw edge on one side of the piping, wrapping it around the remaining side, encasing the cording and raw edges. Stitch across the join ¼" from the raw edge.

4. Place the pillow front and back right sides together. Stitch the edges together on the stitching line of the piping, stitching as close as possible to the piping and leaving an opening on one edge.

5. Turn the cover right side out, clipping corners as needed to make them smooth. Insert the pillow form. Slipstitch the opening closed.

Bill-in-a-Corner Pillow Pattern

Button

Bill
Cut 4

w

w

Color Key

▨	Blue Plaid	▨	Light Brown	▨	Purple
w	White	▨	Tan		

34

SUE-IN-A-CORNER
Pillow

Materials

½ yard of 44"-wide lavender print fabric
    for pillow
⅜ yard of 44"-wide black fabric for piping
Scraps of fabric in these colors: gold
    print, tan, orange, rust/black check,
    and lavender
10" x 10" piece of black felt
Thread to match the fabrics
Embroidery floss in these colors: gray,
    brown, blue, and purple
2 yards of ½"-wide cording
14" pillow form
½"-diameter lavender button
Tracing paper for patterns
Dressmaker's chalk
Water-soluble marking pen

Appliqué the Design

Note: Refer to "Needle-Turn Appliqué" on page 6 for general instructions. Refer to the project photo and pattern for placement.

1. Trace the patterns individually onto tracing paper and cut apart. Referring to the photo and the color key, pin the pattern pieces to the desired fabric and cut out, adding a ¼" seam allowance to all edges.

2. Fold the black felt into quarters and mark the center. Appliqué the fabric pieces for Sue in one corner of the felt square in this order: feet, hands, sleeves, dress, and hat. Repeat at the remaining corners to complete 4 Sue figures.

Embroider the Details

Note: For the embroidery stitches, follow the instructions on page 11. Refer to the photo and pattern for placement.

1. Mark the embroidery lines with a water-soluble pen.

2. Using 2 strands of brown floss, sew running stitches in the crown of the hats. Buttonhole-stitch around each hat. Tack-stitch each sleeve.

3. Using 2 strands of gray floss, chain-stitch the bows between the figures. Sew running stitches across the bottom edges of the dresses. Sew a button in the center of the design.

4. Using 2 strands of purple floss, tack-stitch around the shoes.

Finish the Pillow

1. From the lavender print fabric, cut two 14" x 14" pieces.

2. Trim the black felt to 9¼" x 9¼" with the design centered. Center the black felt square on the right side of one lavender print piece. Pin in place and buttonhole-stitch all edges using 2 strands of blue floss.

3. From the black fabric, cut 1½"-wide bias strips, piecing as needed, to equal at least 2 yards. To make piping, place the cording in the center of the wrong side of the bias strip. Fold the bias strip over the cording and stitch close to the cording using a zipper foot. Trim the seam allowance ¼" from the stitching line. Place the piping on the right side of the pillow front. Begin stitching 1" from end of piping. Stitch with a ¼" seam, rounding corners and clipping the seam allowance as needed. At the end, trim the piping to overlap by 1". Remove the stitching from one end for about 1"; trim the cording so the ends just meet. Fold over the raw edge on one side of the piping, wrapping it around the remaining side, encasing the cording and raw edges. Stitch across the join ¼" from the raw edge.

4. Place the pillow front and back right sides together. Stitch the edges together on the stitching line of the piping, stitching as close as possible to the piping and leaving an opening on one edge.

5. Turn the cover right side out, clipping corners as needed to make them smooth. Insert the pillow form. Slipstitch the opening closed.

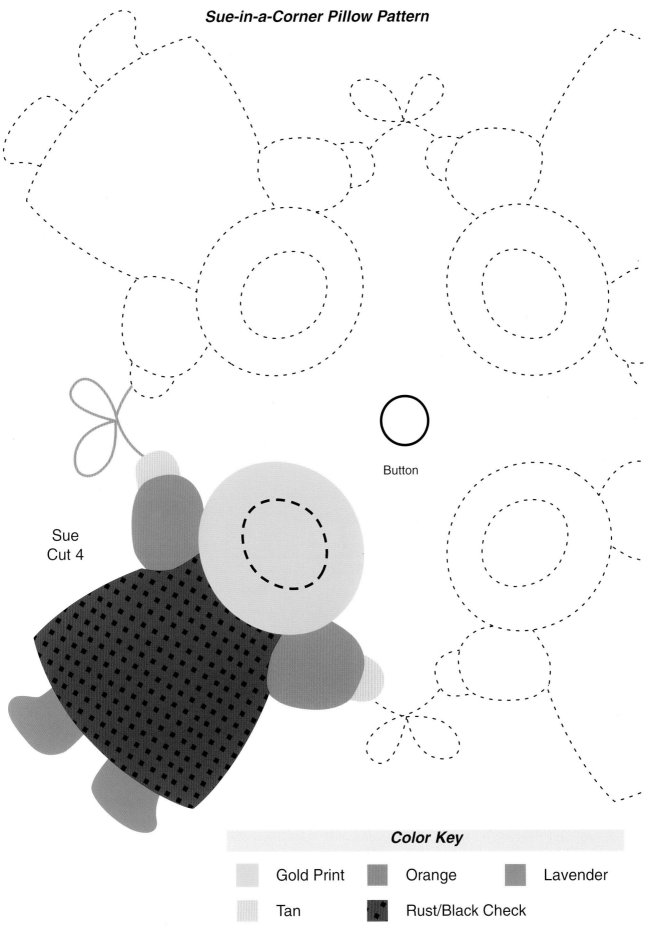

Button

Sue
Cut 4

Color Key

Gold Print   Orange   Lavender

Tan   Rust/Black Check

LAUNDRY DAY
WALL HANGING

Materials

¾ yard of 44"-wide lavender fabric for backing and border

½ yard of 44"-wide gold fabric for background

¼ yard of 44"-wide very light green fabric for grass and tree top

Scraps of cotton fabric in these colors: light green, rust, olive, brown, charcoal print, rose, blue print, tan, blue/tan check, green print, green dot, brown/black print, quilt print, turquoise print, red, turquoise, blue/black print, pink check, beige, white, black print, red/yellow print, brown print, apricot check, lavender, light blue print, red print, tan print, and aqua

Thread to match fabrics

Embroidery floss in these colors: dark blue, tan, and white

White quilting thread

½ yard batting

Tracing paper and pencil

Water-soluble pen

Prepare the Background

1. Trace the patterns individually onto tracing paper and cut apart. Referring to the photo and the color key, pin the pattern pieces to the desired fabric and cut out, adding a ¼" seam allowance to all edges. To make the grass, cut a 4½" x 35" piece of very light green fabric. Referring to the photo and Diagram 1, trim 1 long edge in a gently waving pattern.

2. Cut a 14" x 35" piece of gold fabric. Using the water-soluble pen, mark 1¼" parallel to and inside all edges; this will be the edge of the border.

3. Turn under ¼" on the top edge of the very light green grass piece. Place the grass piece on the gold background, extending it ¼" into the border on the sides and lower edge; pin.

4. Plan the placement of all 3 rainbow pieces; extend the bottom edges of the rainbow under the top edge of the grass. Begin by appliquéing the outside edge only of the apricot check band, then the outside edge of the lavender band, and both edges of the light blue print band.

5. Appliqué the upper edge only of the grass.

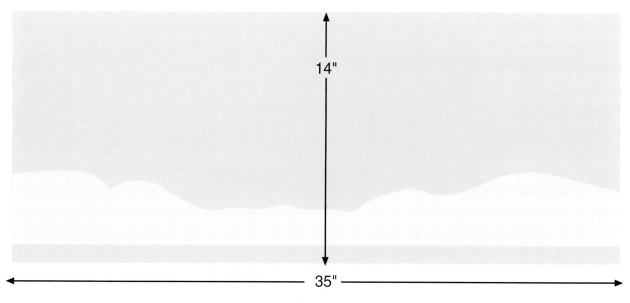

14"

35"

Diagram 1

Appliqué the Design

Note: Refer to "Needle-Turn Appliqué" on page 6 for general instructions. Refer to the project photo and pattern for placement.

1. Begin with the 2 quilts on the clothesline. Place them on the background with the top edges 5½" (without the seam allowance) from the top edge of the gold fabric. Appliqué all edges.

2. Plan the placement for Sue #2. Appliqué her feet and dress. Her hand, sleeve, and hat will be added later.

3. Appliqué the cat body, then its head.

4. Appliqué Sue #4. Appliqué her feet and dress, then her hand, sleeve, and hat.

5. Plan the placement for Sue #3. Appliqué her feet and dress, then appliqué all the edges of the quilt. Appliqué the hand, sleeve, and hat, for Sue #2 and #3.

6. To appliqué Sue #1, begin with the stool. Then follow the sequence in Step 4.

7. To appliqué Sue #5, begin with the stool. Then appliqué her shoes and dress. Appliqué the needlework, hand, sleeve, and hat.

8. To the left of the figures, appliqué the medium green tree top, then its trunk. Appliqué the very light green tree top, then the trunk. To the right of the figures, appliqué the light green tree top, then the trunk. Appliqué the large group of apples, then the 2 individual apples. Appliqué the basket.

9. Appliqué the aqua grass pieces, placing the bottom edges even with the very light green grass piece. Also appliqué the clouds.

Embroider the Details

Note: For the embroidery stitches, follow the instructions on page 11. Refer to the photo and pattern for placement.

1. Mark the embroidery lines with a water-soluble pen.

2. Mark the clothesline. Using 2 strands of dark blue floss, stem-stitch the clothesline and the flower stems. Sew running stitches for the crown of the hat on each Sue. Stem-stitch the embroidery hoop on the needlework. Sew running stitches ¼" below and parallel to the top edge of the apple basket. Satin-stitch the cat's eyes and nose. Backstitch the cat's mouth and legs. Sew running stitches around the cat's face on the body piece.

3. Using 3 strands of white floss, make 6 lazy daisy petals on the flower stems.

4. Using 2 strands of tan floss, satin-stitch the clothespins for the quilts on the line.

Quilt the Wall Hanging

1. Cut a 17" x 38" piece of lavender fabric. Cut a 14" x 35" piece of batting. Center the batting and the design piece over the wrong side of the lavender fabric. Baste.

2. Using white thread, quilt closely around every appliquéd piece. Also quilt lines in the grass, blocks in the center quilt, and lines between the shoes. Use the photo as a guide for grass lines.

3. Fold the lavender fabric to the front over the design piece. Fold under the raw edge to make a 1¼" border on all sides. Slipstitch the edge to the design piece, mitering the corners. Quilt inside the border on the design piece.

Color Key

Very Light Green		Turquoise	
Light Green		Blue/Black Print	
Rust		Pink Check	
Olive		Beige	
Brown		White	
Charcoal Print		Black Print	
Rose		Red/Yellow Print	
Blue Print		Brown Print	
Tan		Apricot Check	
Blue/Tan Check		Lavender	
Green Print		Light Blue Print	
Green Dot		Red Print	
Brown/Black Print		Tan Print	
Quilt Print		Aqua	
Turquoise Print		Medium Red Print	
Red			

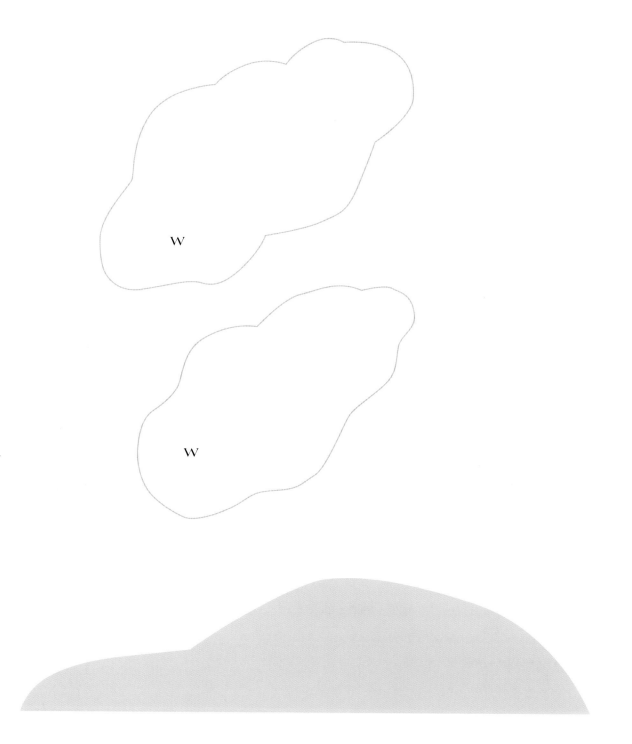

Sue #1

Sue #3

Sue #2

46

Sue #5

W

Sue #4

OVERALL BILL
BIRTH ANNOUNCEMENT

Materials

15" x 21" piece of blue chambray fabric
15" x 21" piece of flannel
Scraps of cotton fabric in these colors: blue
    check, navy blue, red, deep purple,
    purple, lavender, cream print, dark green
    print, rust, yellow-green, light green, tan,
    gold, light blue, and terra cotta
Embroidery floss in these colors: white,
    navy blue, red, purple, gold, bright
    green, green, light green, rust, cream,
    tan, rose, mauve, and light blue
½ yard of paper-backed fusible web
Tracing paper and pencil
Air-soluble marking pen

Prepare the Background

*Note: Refer to "Fused Appliqué" on page 7 for
general instructions.*

1. Fold the blue chambray background
fabric into quarters and mark the center
of each edge. Mark a 9½" x 14" rectangle
in the center of the fabric.

2. Cut a 9½" x 14" piece of tracing paper.
Trace the outside edges of the name frame
and Overall Bill onto the tracing paper.
Cut out the frame and Bill, leaving the rest
of the paper intact. Pin this template over
the background fabric with the outside
edges matching the edges of the marked
rectangle (Diagram 1).

3. Referring to "Preparing the Pattern Pieces"
on page 7, trace the shapes onto fusible
web. When all the pieces have been traced,
pin the overlay to the chambray and leave
in place throughout the appliqué process.

4. Apply the fusible web pieces with the
traced designs to the wrong side of the
appropriate fabric scraps. Cut out the
fabric piece for the name frame. Peel off
the paper backing and place the fabric
frame on the background, fusible side
down, using the overlay as a guide. Fuse.
Cut out the pieces for Overall Bill. Fuse
the shoes, hands, sleeves, overalls, hat, and
hatband (Diagram 2). Remove template.

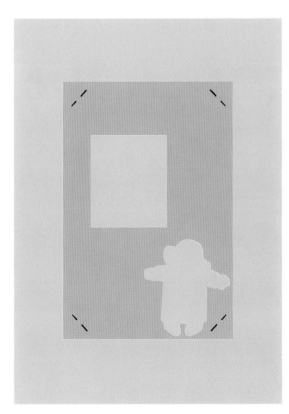

Diagram 1

Diagram 2

Appliqué the Details

Note: Refer to "Needle-Turn Appliqué" on page 6 for general instructions. Refer to the project photo and pattern for placement.

1. Cut out and fuse the background square for the fan block above the right corner of the frame, and the rectangle at the right edge of the design. Cut out and fuse the clouds.

2. Cut out and fuse the fan pieces in the quilt block. Then cut out and fuse the curved band, followed by the fan corner piece of the quilt block.

3. Cut out and fuse the scalloped pieces behind the hearts in the upper left corner, then cut and fuse the hearts. Cut out and fuse the scalloped border above the hearts.

4. Cut out and fuse the tree top, then the trunk. Cut out and fuse the corners above the tree.

5. Cut out and fuse the crazy quilt pieces in the space to the left of the frame.

6. Cut out and fuse the stem and leaves to the flower pot, then the flower and the pot. Cut out and fuse the zigzag edge to the right of the flower pot.

7. Cut out and fuse the rectangle at the left edge in the lower block, then fuse the 4 corners. Cut out and fuse the sheep's legs and face, followed by its body.

8. Cut out and fuse the smaller wing of both birds. Then cut out and fuse the body, followed by the larger wing.

Embroider the Details

Note: For the embroidery stitches, follow the instructions on page 11. Refer to the photo and pattern for placement.

1. Write or transfer the name and birth date, using the alphabet on page 60. Stem-stitch the name, using 1 strand of navy blue floss. Sew running stitches in a zigzag in the center, using 1 strand of gold floss. Stem-stitch the date, using 1 strand of red floss. Make a French knot to dot the *i*.

2. Using 2 strands of white floss, buttonhole-stitch the bottom edge of the scalloped piece and the edges of Bill's sleeves. Also buttonhole-stitch in the lower part of the crazy quilt block as shown in the photo. Sew running stitches to outline the blocks for the scalloped piece, the hearts, the tree, and the flower pot. Sew running stitches along the right and bottom edges of the bottom block, indica-ted by a broken gray line. Backstitch the left edge of the crazy quilt block, some of the lines in the crazy quilt block, and the 2 vertical lines below the right-side rec-tangle. Tack-stitch the edges of the heart background, scalloped edges, and clouds. Make French knots in Bill's hatband.

3. Using 2 strands of navy blue floss, backstitch lines in the crazy quilt block. Sew running stitches inside the edges of the hearts. Stem-stitch the outline of each fan piece in the fan block and the pocket on Bill's overalls. Buttonhole-stitch around Bill's hat and the sheep's body. Make French knots for the bird's eyes. Stem-stitch the bird's legs.

4. Using 2 strands of bright green floss, buttonhole-stitch around the edges of the tree top.

5. Using 2 strands of rust floss, buttonhole-stitch around the edges of the tree trunk. Satin-stitch the birds' beaks.

6. Using 2 strands of red floss, tack-stitch the arc and corner pieces of the fan block, and around the birds' wings. Buttonhole-stitch around the flower.

7. Using 2 strands of purple floss, back-stitch inside the edges of the corner pieces of the tree block and the birds' bodies.

8. Using 2 strands of green floss, sew running stitches in the flower stem and around the edges of the leaves. Buttonhole-stitch around Bill's overalls.

9. Buttonhole-stitch the inside edge of the frame, using 2 strands of rose floss.

10. Buttonhole-stitch the outside edge of the frame, using 2 strands of cream floss. Also buttonhole-stitch the outside edge of the flower pot. Backstitch the rim of the flower pot.

11. Buttonhole-stitch the outside edges of the corner pieces and the rectangle in the lower block as shown, using 2 strands of light green floss.

12. Using 1 strand of light blue floss, make French knots in the clouds, wrapping the floss around the needle once. Stem-stitch between the sheep's legs. Using 2 strands of light blue floss, tack-stitch the edges of the sheep's legs and face.

13. Using 2 strands of mauve floss, button-hole-stitch in the crazy quilt block, and cross-stitch 1 seam.

Frame the Design

Have a professional framer frame the piece, padding with the piece of flannel.

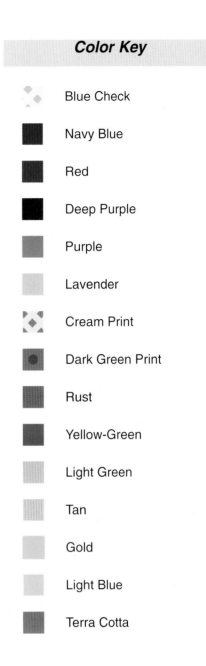

Color Key

- Blue Check
- Navy Blue
- Red
- Deep Purple
- Purple
- Lavender
- Cream Print
- Dark Green Print
- Rust
- Yellow-Green
- Light Green
- Tan
- Gold
- Light Blue
- Terra Cotta

Mary
Claire
Boerens
Nov 17,
19XX

SUNBONNET SUE
BIRTH ANNOUNCEMENT

Materials

15" x 21" piece of yellow fabric

15" x 21" piece of flannel

Scraps of cotton in these colors: gold, gold print, rose, medium blue print, lavender, pink, light blue print, green print, rust, apricot check, light green, white, terra cotta, light green print, tan, blue-gray, and purple

Embroidery floss in these colors: dark aqua, rose, gold, purple, white, light green, rust, lavender, medium blue, and apricot

½ yard of paper-backed fusible web

Tracing paper

Pencil

Air-soluble marking pen

Prepare the Background

Complete steps 1 through 4 of "Prepare the Background" on page 51, substituting the yellow fabric for the blue chambray and substituting Sue for Bill. Cut out and fuse Sue's hands and legs, then the shoes, dress, hat, and hatband.

Appliqué the Details

Note: Refer to "Needle-Turn Appliqué" on page 6 for general instructions. Refer to the project photo and pattern for placement.

Complete steps 1 through 8 of "Appliqué the Details" on page 52.

Embroider the Details

Note: For the embroidery stitches, follow the instructions on page 11. Refer to the photo and pattern for placement.

1. Write or transfer the name and birth date, using the alphabet and numbers on page 60. Stem-stitch the name, using 1 strand of dark aqua floss. Sew running stitches in the center, using 1 strand of purple floss. Stem-stitch the date, using 1 strand of rose floss. Make a French knot to dot the *i*.

2. Using 2 strands of gold floss, buttonhole-stitch the bottom edge of the scalloped piece. Tack-stitch the edges of the heart background, scalloped edges, and crazy quilt pieces. Satin-stitch the birds' beaks.

3. Using 2 strands of rose floss, buttonhole-stitch in the lower part of the crazy quilt block as shown in the photo. Sew running stitches to outline the blocks for the scalloped piece, the hearts, the tree, and the flower pot. Sew running stitches along the right and bottom edges of the bottom block. Backstitch the left edge of the crazy quilt block, some of the lines in the crazy quilt block, and the 2 vertical lines below the right-side rectangle.

4. Using 2 strands of dark aqua floss, buttonhole-stitch in the crazy quilt block. Also cross-stitch 1 seam.

5. Using 2 strands of mauve floss, sew running stitches inside the edges of the hearts. Buttonhole-stitch around Sue's hat and the sheep's body. Make French knots in Sue's hatband. Make French knots for the birds' eyes. Stem-stitch the bird's legs.

6. Buttonhole-stitch with 2 strands of light green floss around the edges of the tree top. Sew running stitches in the flower stem, around the edges of the leaves, and on the inside edges of the rectangle on the right edge of the design.

7. Using 2 strands of rust floss, buttonhole-stitch around the edges of the tree trunk and the inside edge of the name frame.

8. Using 2 strands of apricot floss, stem-stitch the outline of each fan piece. In the tree block, backstitch the inside edges of the corner pieces. Buttonhole-stitch the outside edge of the frame block, the upper right corner triangle of the bottom block, Sue's dress, and the outside edge of the flower pot. Backstitch the rim of the flower pot.

9. Using 2 strands of lavender floss, buttonhole-stitch the outside edges of the 3 remaining corner pieces and the rectangle in the lower block. Tack-stitch the edges of the sheep's legs, sheep's face, and the birds' wings. Using 1 strand of lavender floss, make French knots in the clouds. Stem-stitch between the sheep's legs.

10. Using 2 strands of white floss, sew running stitches around the edges of the white background in the fan block. Tack-stitch the edges of the arc piece and the corner piece in the fan block.

11. Using 2 strands of medium blue floss, backstitch inside the birds' bodies.

Frame the Design

Have a professional framer frame the piece, padding the design piece with the piece of flannel.

Color Key

	Gold
	Gold Print
	Dark Gold Print
	Rose
	Medium Blue Print
	Lavender
	Pink
	Light Blue Print
	Green Print
	Rust
	Apricot Check
	Light Green
w	White
	Terra Cotta
	Light Green Print
	Tan
	Blue-Gray
	Purple

ABCDEF

GHIJKL

MNOPQR

STUVWXYZ

abcdefghijk

lmnopqrst

uvwxyz

0123456789

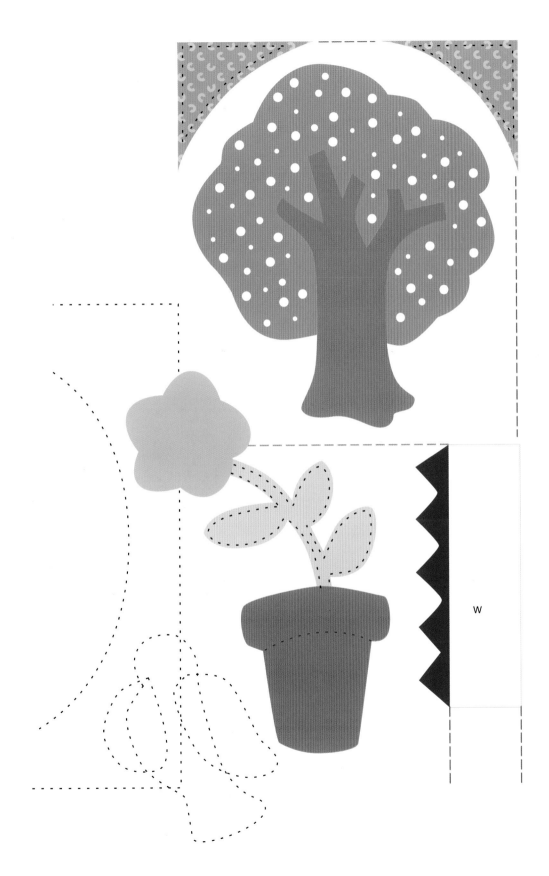

Sunbonnet Sue Birth Announcement Pattern

W

FLOWERPOTS
PILLOW

Materials

½ yard of 44"-wide blue print
12" x 12" piece of yellow for
    background
Scraps of cotton fabric in these colors:
    lavender, light green, and rust
Thread to match fabrics
Embroidery floss in these colors:
    lavender, light green, and rust
14" pillow form
Tracing paper for patterns
Water-soluble marking pen

Appliqué the Design

Note: Refer to "Needle-Turn Appliqué" on page 6 for general instructions. Refer to the project photo and pattern for placement.

1. Trace the patterns individually onto tracing paper. Referring to the photo and the color keys, pin the pattern pieces to the desired fabric and cut out 4 of each, adding a ¼" seam allowance to all edges.

2. Fold the background square into quarters; mark the center and crease the folds (Diagram 1). Mark the placement for each flower pot, placing the bottom ¼" from the creased line and 1" from the brim of the nearest flowerpot; see the pattern. Mark placement for the flowers 3" from the center on each crease line.

3. Appliqué the stems onto the background. Appliqué the flowers, then the flowerpots.

Diagram 1

Embroider the Details

Note: For the embroidery stitches, follow the instructions on page 11. Refer to the photo and pattern for placement.

1. Buttonhole-stitch around the edges of the flowers, using 2 strands of lavender floss.

2. Using 2 strands of rust floss, buttonhole-stitch around the edges of the flowerpots. Backstitch the edge of the rim.

3. Sew running stitches on the stems and leaves, using 2 strands of light green floss.

Make the Pillow

1. Trim the yellow background to 11½" x 11½", with the design centered.

2. From the blue print fabric, cut the following: 1 piece, 14" x 14"; and 4 strips, 1¾" x 16".

3. Use a pin to mark the center of each edge of the background. Also mark the centers of 1 long edge of each strip. With right sides together and raw edges even, match the center of a strip with the center of one edge of the background. Using a ¼" seam, stitch the strip to the background, starting and stopping ¼" from corners; backstitch. Repeat with the remaining strips.

4. Miter the 4 corners, referring to the instructions on page 9.

5. Place the pillow front and back right sides together. Stitch the edges together, using a ¼" seam and leaving an opening in 1 edge.

6. Turn the pillow cover right side out, clipping corners as needed to make them smooth. Insert the pillow form. Slipstitch the opening closed.

Color Key

▓	Light Green
▓	Lavender
▓	Rust

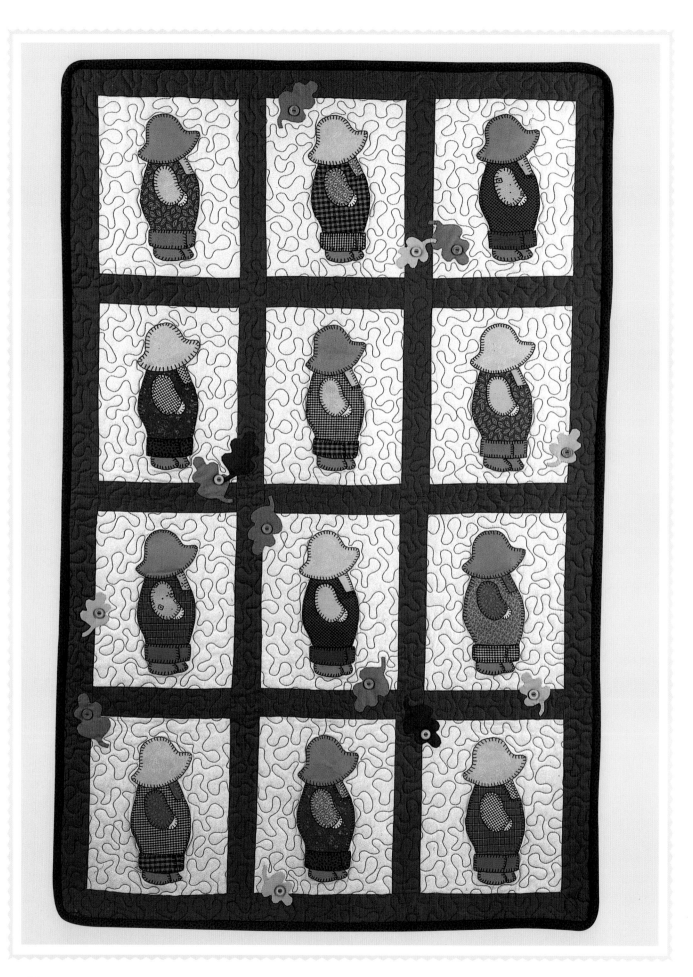

OVERALL BILL
QUILT

Materials

2¾ yards of 44"-wide brown/black print fabric for backing and binding

1½ yards of 44"-wide brown fabric for sashing and border

1 yard of 44"-wide lavender print fabric for block backgrounds

Scraps of cotton fabric in these colors: gold, dark gold, blue-green, tan, brown print, olive, gray/black check, gray print, tan/black check, rust/black print, tan print, rust, purple print, red/cream check, navy print, turquoise, blue plaid, blue, green print, rust print, light green, medium green, dark green

Thread to match fabrics

Black embroidery floss

1½ yards of 44"-wide polyester fleece

12 gold ⅝"-diameter buttons

Tracing paper and pencil

Air-soluble marking pen

Appliqué the Blocks

Note: Refer to "Needle-Turn Appliqué" on page 6 for general instructions.

1. Trace the patterns individually onto tracing paper. Referring to the photo, pin the pattern pieces to the desired fabrics and cut out, adding a ¼" seam allowance to all edges.

2. Cut out 5 small light green leaves, 6 large medium green leaves, and 2 large dark green leaves; set the leaves aside.

3. From the lavender print fabric, cut 12 pieces, 9" x 11". Using the air-soluble pen, mark the vertical center of each.

4. For each block, appliqué the shoes 1" from the bottom edge of the block, centering them over the vertical line. Then appliqué the shirt, overalls, and cuffs. Appliqué the hand, sleeve, and hat, noting their placement in relation to the center line. Make 12 blocks.

Embroider the Blocks

Note: For the embroidery stitches, follow the instructions on page 11. Refer to the photo and pattern for placement.

Mark the inside edges of the left shoe and left cuff. Buttonhole-stitch around the edges of all the pieces in each Bill figure, using 2 strands of black floss. Include the inside edges of the cuff and shoe.

Assemble the Quilt

1. From the brown fabric, cut 2 pieces, 2¼" x 53" and 2 pieces, 2¼" x 36", for the border. Cut 2 pieces, 2¼" x 48" and 9 pieces, 2¼" x 9", for the sashing. From the brown/black print fabric, cut 3"-wide bias strips, piecing as needed to equal 5 yards.

2. Lay out the blocks in the desired pattern. Sew 2¼" x 9" sashing pieces to the lower edge of each block in the first 3 rows (Diagram 1). Then join the blocks to make 3 vertical rows (Diagram 2).

3. Sew 2¼" x 48" pieces to the right edge of the first and second rows (Diagram 3). Then join the three rows. Trim any excess sashing.

4. Use pins to mark the center of each edge of the quilt top and the center of one long edge of each border piece. With right sides together and raw edges even, match the center of a short border piece with the top edge of the quilt. Using a ¼" seam, stitch the border piece to the quilt top, starting and stopping ¼" from each corner of the top. Repeat with each edge and the remaining border pieces.

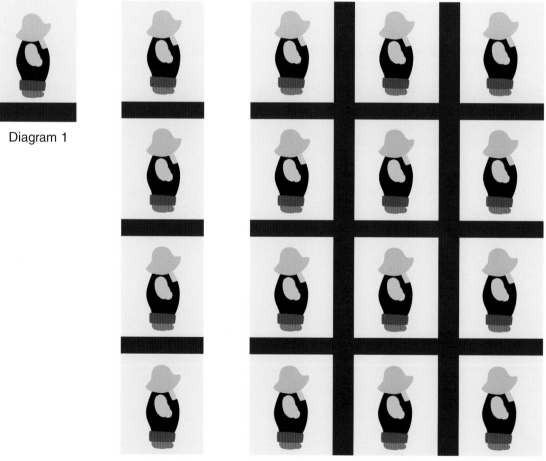

Diagram 1

Diagram 2

Diagram 3

5. Miter the 4 corners (Diagram 4 and close-up view), referring to the instructions on page 9.

6. Place the backing fabric on a flat surface, wrong side up. Layer the fleece over the backing. Center the quilt top right side up over the fleece; baste. Using brown thread, machine quilt the blocks, sashing, and borders in a meandering random pattern except where the appliqué designs sit.

7. Fold the bias strips in half lengthwise; press. With the raw edges matching the raw edges of the quilt, stitch the bias to the right side of the quilt top, gently rounding each corner. Fold to the back and slipstitch.

8. Appliqué the leaves to the quilt, referring to the photo for placement. Sew buttons on some of the leaves.

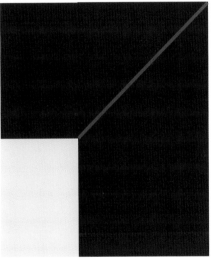

Diagram 4 close-up

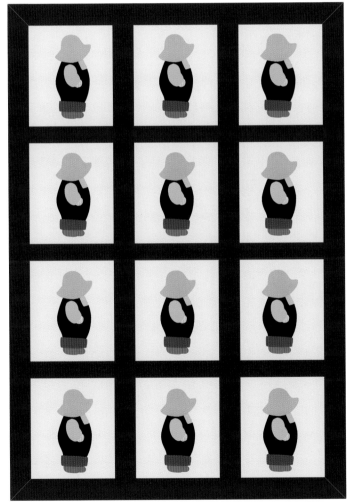

Diagram 4

74

SUNBONNET SUE
QUILT

Materials

2¾ yards of 44"-wide light blue print fabric for backing and binding

1½ yards of 44"-wide medium blue fabric for sashing and border

1 yard of 44"-wide pink fabric for block backgrounds

Scraps of cotton fabric in these colors: brown, light rust check, tan, cream, blue print, navy blue, purple, pink, red/yellow print, blue print, light green, yellow print, navy blue check, lavender print, red print, blue/white check, gray/black check, tan print, rose, and green

Thread to match fabrics

Black embroidery floss

1½ yards 44"-wide polyester fleece

21 white ⅜"-diameter buttons

Tracing paper

Pencil

Air-soluble marking pen

Appliqué the Block

Note: Refer to "Needle-Turn Appliqué" on page 6 for general instructions.

1. Trace the patterns individually onto tracing paper. Referring to the photo, pin the pattern pieces to the desired fabrics and cut out, adding a ¼" seam allowance to all edges.

2. Cut out 7 flowers and 14 leaves; set the flowers and leaves aside.

3. From the pink fabric, cut 12 pieces, 9" x 11". Using the air-soluble pen, mark the vertical center of each.

4. For each block, appliqué the shoes 1" from the bottom edge of the block, centering them over the vertical line. Then appliqué the skirt, apron, and hand. Appliqué the bodice, sleeve, and hat, noting their placement in relation to the center line. Make 12 blocks.

Embroider the Blocks

Note: For the embroidery stitches, follow the instructions on page 11. Refer to the photo and pattern for placement.

Mark the inside edge of the right shoe and the upper sleeve. Buttonhole-stitch around the edges of all the pieces in each Sue figure, using 2 strands of black floss. Include the inside edge of the shoe and the upper sleeve.

Assemble the Quilt

1. From the medium blue fabric, cut 2 pieces, 2¼" x 53", and 2 pieces, 2¼" x 36", for the border. Cut 2 pieces, 2¼" x 48", and 9 pieces, 2¼" x 9", for the sashing. From the blue print binding fabric, cut 3"-wide bias strips, piecing as needed to equal 5¼ yards.

2. Lay out the blocks in the desired pattern. Sew 2¼" x 9" sashing pieces to the lower edge of each block in the first 3 rows (Diagram 1). Then join the blocks to make 3 vertical rows (Diagram 2).

3. Sew 2¼" x 48" pieces to the right edge of the first and second rows (Diagram 3). Then join the three rows. Trim any excess sashing.

4. Use pins to mark the center of each edge of the quilt top and the center of one long edge of each border piece. With right sides together and raw edges even, match the center of a short border piece with the top edge of the quilt. Using a ¼" seam, stitch the border piece to the quilt top, starting and stopping ¼" from each corner of the top. Repeat with the remaining border pieces.

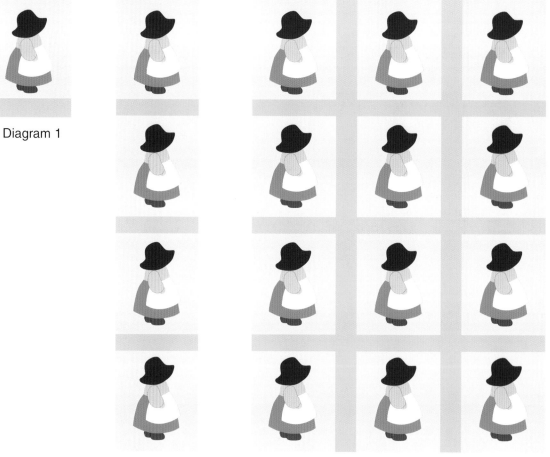

Diagram 1

Diagram 2

Diagram 3

5. Miter the 4 corners (Diagram 4 and close-up view), referring to the instructions on page 9.

6. Place the backing fabric on a flat surface, wrong side up. Layer the fleece over the backing. Center the quilt top right side up over the fleece; baste. Using light blue thread machine-quilt the blocks, sashing, and borders in a random meandering pattern except where the appliqué designs sit.

7. Fold the bias strips in half lengthwise; press. With the raw edges matching the raw edges of the quilt, stitch the bias to the right side of the quilt top, gently rounding each corner. Fold to the back and slipstitch.

8. Appliqué the flowers and leaves to the quilt, referring to the photo. Sew 3 buttons to the center of each flower.

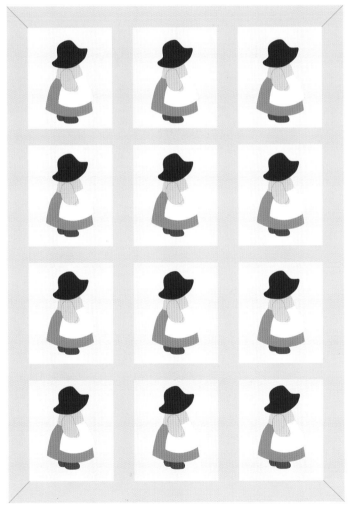

Diagram 4

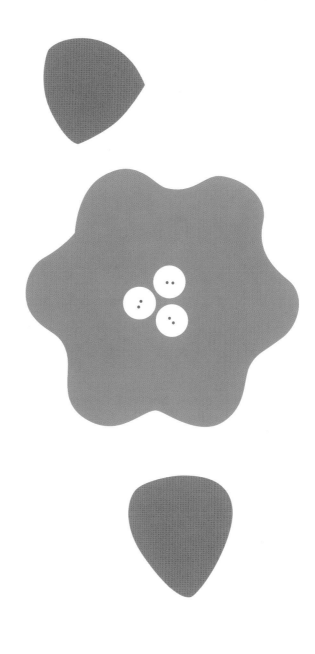

80

DAYS OF THE WEEK
QUILT

Materials

3½ yards of 44"-wide lavender print fabric for sashing, borders, backing, and binding

¼ yard of 44"-wide gray print fabric for corner squares

¼ yard each of 44"-wide pale blue and light green fabrics for block backgrounds

7" x 16¼" piece of light blue fabric for block background

10" x 16 " piece of blue/tan check fabric for block background

8" x 10" piece of medium blue print for block background

Scraps of cotton fabric in these colors: orange check, gold print, gold, turquoise, tan print, brown print, tan, white, brown, black, blue-green print, dark green, bright green, light brown, rose, lavender, navy blue, yellow, blue plaid, pale lavender print, red print, tan/brown print, green, red/navy check, black/tan check, tan stripe, orange, blue-gray print, brick red, rust, blue print, medium brown, green print, red/yellow print, and yellow/blue check

Thread to match fabrics

Embroidery floss in these colors: charcoal, dark green, dark brown, brown, cream, orange, navy blue, blue, gold, purple, lavender, and dark red

1¼ yards of 44"-wide polyester fleece

Tracing paper for patterns

Air-soluble marking pen

General Instructions

Note: Refer to "Needle-Turn Appliqué" on page 6 for general instructions.

Working with one block at a time, trace the patterns individually onto tracing paper. Referring to the photo and the color key, pin the pattern pieces to the desired fabrics and cut them out, adding a ¼" seam allowance to all edges.

Prepare the backgrounds for the blocks according to the individual instructions. The Sunday background is 10½" x 16¼" and all of the others are 8" x 10½" before assembly.

Sunday Block

1. To make the background, cut a 4½" x 16¼" piece of light green fabric for the grass. Referring to the photo and Diagram 1, trim one long edge in a loosely scalloped pattern. Cut a 3" x 7¼" piece of blue-green print fabric. Referring to the photo and Diagram 1, trim one long edge in a gently waving pattern. Pin the blue-green and light green pieces to the 7" x 16¼" light blue fabric, adjusting as necessary. Appliqué the top edge of the blue-green print, then the light green piece. Trim excess light blue fabric from behind the light green fabric.

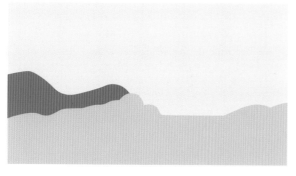

Diagram 1

	Color Key
	Orange Check
	Gold Print
	Gold
	Turquoise
	Brown Print
	Tan Print
w	White
	Brown
	Black
	Dark Green
	Bright Green
	Blue

2. Appliqué the pale blue cloud to the center of the sky piece, with the top edge 1¼" from the top of the background.

3. Mark the placement of the bushes, the church, and the Sue figure. Appliqué the dark green bush.

4. Appliqué the right side of the church, then the roof. Appliqué the steeple, beginning with the bottom piece and setting aside the top brown piece. Appliqué the church front, the path, and the door. Appliqué the bright green bush.

5. Appliqué Sue's shoes and dress, then her hand, sleeve, and hat. Appliqué the three small flowers.

Sunday - Worship

Bushes
(see diagram
on page 82)

Lawn
(see diagram
on page 82)

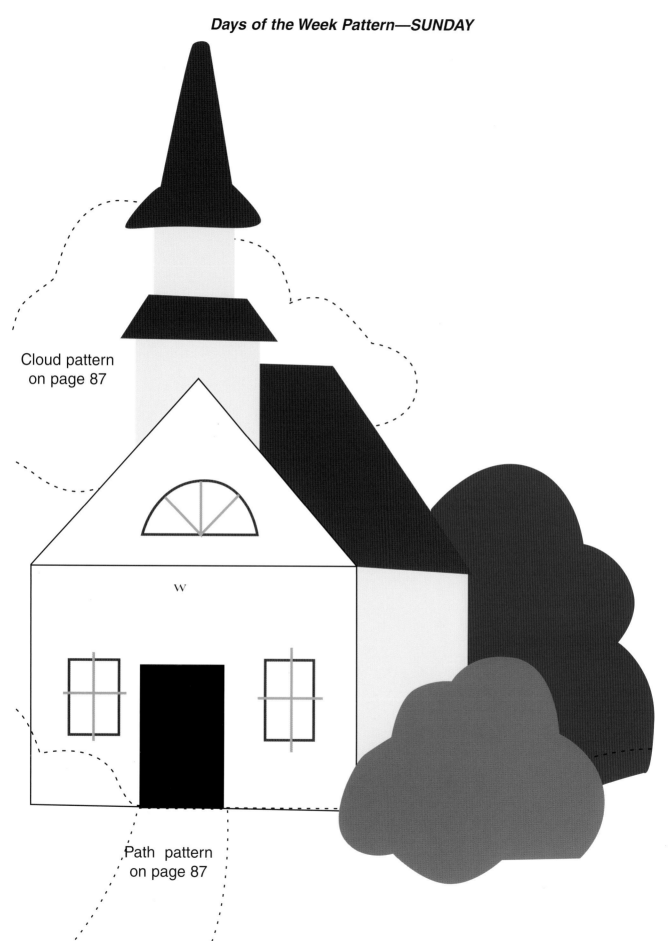

Cloud pattern
on page 87

W

Path pattern
on page 87

Path

Cloud

Monday Block

1. To make the background, cut an 8" x 9" piece of blue/tan check and a 2" x 8" piece of light brown fabric. Sew the 8" edges together using a ¼" seam.

2. Mark the placement for the stool, the framed pieced, and the Sue figure. Appliqué the blue-green stool. Appliqué the back piece of the bucket, then the white laundry and the front of the bucket.

3. Appliqué Sue's shoes, dress, and apron, then appliqué the hand, sleeve, hat, and flower.

4. Appliqué the navy blue frame, then the yellow background and the red heart.

Monday - Wash

Color Key

Gold	Lavender	Blue-Green Print	Navy Blue	w	White
Tan	Rose	Turquoise	Yellow		Brick Red

89

Tuesday Block

1. To make the background, cut an 8" x 9" piece of blue/tan check and a 2" x 8" piece of tan/brown print. Sew the 8" edges together.

2. Mark the placement of the ironing board, the window, and the Sue figure. Appliqué the ironing board and the iron. Baste the pale blue window to the background, then appliqué the green sash over it.

3. Appliqué Sue's shoes, dress, and apron, then the hand, sleeve, hat, and flower.

Tuesday - Iron

Color Key

Turquoise	Blue Plaid	Gold	Rose	Red
Pale Lavender Print	w White	Green	Pale Blue	Brown

Wednesday Block

1. To make the background for both blocks, cut 2 pieces of pale blue fabric 9" x 10½" and 2 pieces of light green fabric 3½" x 9". Referring to the photo and Diagram 2, work with both pieces together and trim one long edge of the light green pieces in a gently waving pattern. Align the lower edges of the pale blue rectangles with the lower edges of the light green grass pieces. Appliqué the top edges of the light green pieces to the pale blue pieces; trim excess light blue fabric from behind the green grass. Appliqué th clouds in place.

2. Cut a 1¼" x 10½" piece of lavender print fabric for sashing. Sew the two background pieces to the sashing piece.

3. Mark the placement of the pole, the Sue figure, the clothing, the cat, and the trees.

4. Appliqué the pole, noting that it is not straight. Appliqué the clothes on the line. Appliqué the light green tree tops. Trim excess light blue fabric from behind the light green fabric, then appliqué the tree trunks.

5. Appliqué the chair. Appliqué Sue's shoes and dress. Then appliqué the white laundry, hands, and sleeves, noting that the grain of the fabric on the upper sleeve is not the same as the lower sleeve. Appliqué the hat and flower.

6. Appliqué the cat.

Color Key

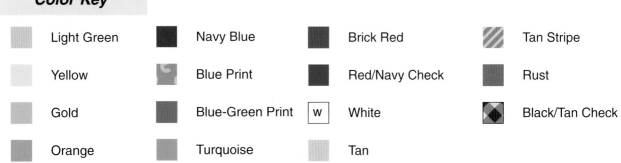

	Light Green		Navy Blue		Brick Red		Tan Stripe
	Yellow		Blue Print		Red/Navy Check		Rust
	Gold		Blue-Green Print	w	White		Black/Tan Check
	Orange		Turquoise		Tan		

Wednesday

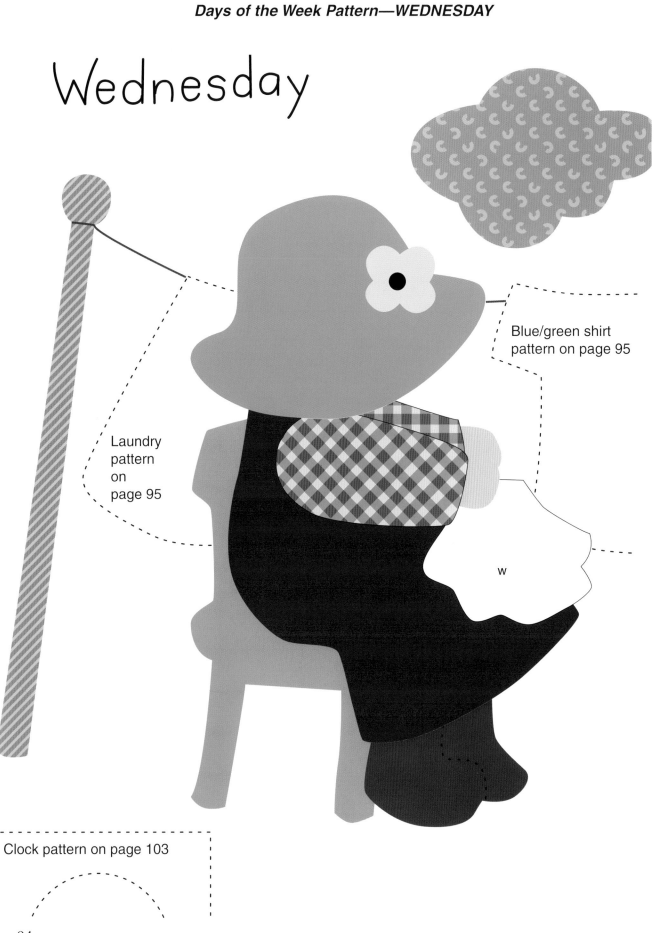

Blue/green shirt
pattern on page 95

Laundry
pattern
on
page 95

w

Clock pattern on page 103

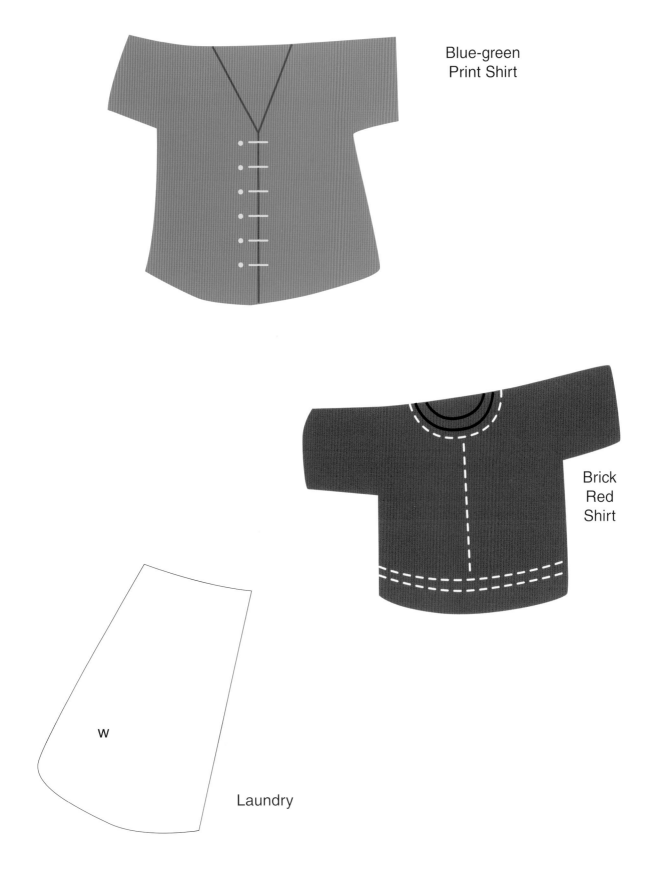

Blue-green
Print Shirt

Brick
Red
Shirt

W

Laundry

Mend

Brick Red Shirt
pattern on page 95

Thursday Block

1. To make the background, cut 1 of each of the following pieces: red/yellow print, 3½" x 8"; navy blue, 2" x 3¼"; light green, 2" x 2"; lavender, 2" x 3" and 3¼" x 6½"; orange check, 4" x 4 ¾"; blue print, 2½" x 5"; and black/tan check, 3¾"x 8". Using ¼" seams, sew the orange check to the blue print, aligning the bottom edges (Diagram 3). Then sew the large lavender piece to the bottom edge (Diagram 4). Sew the navy blue, light green, and small lavender pieces in a strip, then sew the pieced strip to the first group, aligning the bottom edges (Diagram 5).

2. On the black/tan check strip, mark 1" from the upper left corner. Cut a straight line from the mark to the upper right corner (Diagram 6). Lap the check fabric over the lavender fabric. Sew along the diagonal (Diagram 7).

3. Mark the skyline on the pieced section (Diagram 8). Cut ¼" outside the mark, then appliqué the pieced section to the red/yellow print.

4. Mark the placement of the Sue figure. Appliqué Sue's shoes and dress. Appliqué the bread and squash, then the basket, hand and sleeve. Appliqué the hat and flower.

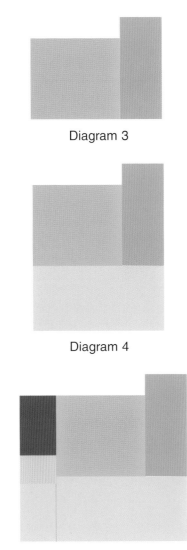

Diagram 3

Diagram 4

Diagram 5

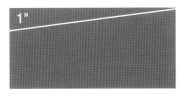

Diagram 6

Diagram 7

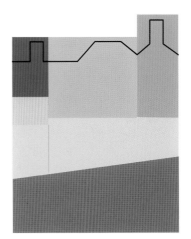

Diagram 8

Color Key

■ Navy	■ Medium Brown	■ Yellow
■ Green Print	■ Brick Red	■ Gold
■ Turquoise	■ Tan	▨ Tan Stripe

Thursday - Shop

Friday Block

1. To make the background, cut an 8" x 8¾" piece of medium blue print and a 2¼" x 8" piece of yellow/blue check fabric. Sew the 8" edges together, using a ¼" seam.

2. Mark the placement of the rug, the clock, and the Sue figure. Appliqué the border of the rug, then the rug center.

3. Appliqué Sue's right hand and right sleeve. (The duster and clock will be appliquéd when the quilt top is assembled.)

4. Appliqué Sue's shoes, dress, and apron. Then appliqué the left hand, left sleeve, hat, and flower.

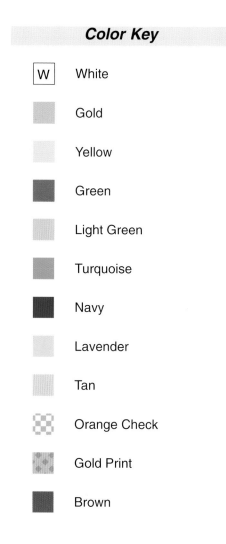

	Color Key
W	White
	Gold
	Yellow
	Green
	Light Green
	Turquoise
	Navy
	Lavender
	Tan
	Orange Check
	Gold Print
	Brown

Clock pattern on page 103

Friday - Clean

Rug pattern on page 103

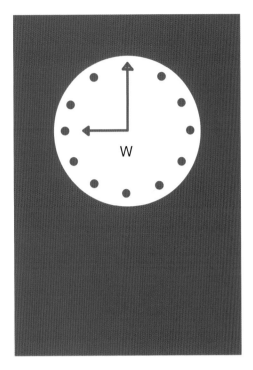

Saturday Block

1. To make the background, cut an 8" x 8½" piece of pale blue and a 2½" x 8" piece of light green fabric. Sew the 8" edges together, using a ¼" seam. Cut 8 pieces of green and 8 pieces of lavender fabric, each 2" x 2". Make a checkerboard, using ¼" seams. Appliqué the checkerboard to the background, placing the top edge 1½" from the top edge of the block.

2. Mark the placement of the Sue figure.

3. Appliqué Sue's shoes, skirt, and apron. Appliqué the hands, arms, and dish, then the hat and flower.

Saturday - Bake

Color Key

Rose

Yellow

Lavender

Brick Red

Navy

Turquoise

Orange Check

Green

w White

105

Embroider the Blocks

Note: For the embroidery stitches, follow the instructions on page 11. Refer to the photo and pattern for placement.

1. On each block, use 2 strands of charcoal floss to buttonhole-stitch around the hat. Make a ¼"-wide spider stitch in the center of the flowers. On the Sunday block, stem-stitch the flower stems.

2. On each block, mark the lettering and backstitch using 2 strands of dark brown floss. Use French knots to dot the *i*'s.

3. On the Sunday block, use 1 strand of dark brown floss to backstitch the windows of the church and the roofline across the front of the church. Using 2 strands of blue floss, stem-stitch the lines on the windows. Using 2 strands of orange floss, cross-stitch the waistline on Sue's dress. Using 1 strand of cream floss, make French knots on the cloud.

4. On the Monday block, use 2 strands of gold floss to cross-stitch the bottom edge of Sue's apron. Using 2 strands of lavender floss, satin-stitch the top band of Sue's apron.

5. On the Tuesday block, use 2 strands of navy blue floss to cross-stitch the bottom edge of Sue's apron. Using 2 strands of lavender floss, satin-stitch the top band of Sue's apron. Using 2 strands of dark brown floss, satin-stitch the bottom of the iron.

6. On the Wednesday block, use 2 strands of navy blue floss to satin-stitch the cat's nose and backstitch its mouth. Again using 2 strands of navy blue floss, backstitch the neckline and front of the blue-green shirt, and stem-stitch the clothesline. Using 2 strands of brown floss, satin-stitch the spots on the cat, then stem-stitch the lines for the cat's legs and neck. Using 1 strand of brown floss, long-stitch the buttonholes on the blue-green shirt; make French knots for buttons. Using 1 strand of navy blue floss, sew running stitches just under the cat's neck. Use 1 strand of charcoal floss to backstitch its whiskers. Using 1 strand of dark red floss, backstitch the neckline

on the red shirt and sew running stitches between Sue's feet. Using 1 strand of cream floss, backstitch the lines on the red shirt.

7. On the Thursday block, use 1 strand of dark red floss to cross-stitch the waistline of Sue's dress. Using 2 strands of purple floss, satin-stitch the windows on the blue print building as shown in Diagram 9.

8. On the Friday block, use 2 strands of gold floss to cross-stitch the bottom edge of Sue's apron. Using 2 strands of dark green floss, satin-stitch the top band of Sue's apron. Using 2 strands of navy blue floss, satin-stitch the duster handle.

9. On the Saturday block, use 1 strand of navy blue floss to cross-stitch along the bottom edge of Sue's apron. Using 2 strands of purple floss, stem-stitch the hearts on the quilt. Using 2 strands of dark brown floss, satin-stitch the bottom of the dish.

Assemble the Quilt

1. From the lavender print fabric, cut 1 piece, 35" x 42", for the backing. Cut 2 pieces, 5½" x 32", and 2 pieces, 5½" x 24½", for the borders; cut 2 pieces, 1¼" x 24½", and 4 pieces, 1¼" x 10 ½", for the sashing. Cut 3"-wide bias strips for the binding, piecing as needed to equal 5½ yards. From the gray print fabric, cut 4 squares, 5½" x 5½", for the corner squares.

2. Lay out the blocks. Sew the short sashing strips between the blocks to make 3 rows (Diagram 9). Then join the rows with the long sashing strips.

3. Appliqué the top piece of the church steeple. In the Friday block, appliqué the clock and clock face, then the duster and upper part of the handle.

4. Use pins to mark the center of each edge of the quilt top and the center of one long edge of each border piece. With right sides together and raw edges even, match the center of a short border piece with the top edge of the quilt. Using a ¼" seam, stitch the border piece to the quilt top. Repeat at bottom edge.

5. Stitch corner squares to each end of the side border pieces. With right sides together and raw edges even, match the center of the border piece with the side edge of the quilt. Using a ¼" seam, stitch the border to the side edge of the quilt. Repeat on the remaining side.

6. Place the backing fabric on a flat surface, wrong side up. Layer the fleece over the backing. Center the quilt top right side up over the fleece; baste. Using lavender thread, quilt in a random pattern all the blocks, sashing and borders except where the appliqué design sits.

7. Fold the bias strips in half lengthwise; press. (On the quilt in the photo, the wrong side of the lavender print fabric is used for the border and sashing, but the right side, which has a small white pattern, is used for the backing and binding.) With the raw edges matching the raw edges of the quilt top, stitch the bias to the right side of the quilt top, mitering each corner as on page 10. Fold to the back and slipstitch in place.

Diagram 9

107

FOUR SEASONS
QUILT

Materials

1 yard of 44"-wide woven navy blue plaid fabric for backing and border

8½" x 13" piece of dark blue print fabric for the winter block background

8½" x 9½" piece of orange check fabric for the fall block background

7½" x 10½" piece of light blue print fabric for the spring block background

8½" x 9" piece of green print for summer block border

8½" x 9" piece of blue fabric for the summer block background

Scraps of cotton fabric in these colors: blue/tan print, dark brown, navy blue, tan, medium green, rose, light green, white, lavender, light brown, gold print, turquoise, bright green print, orange check, yellow, rust/black print, light rust, dark rust, orange, orange print, gold, blue print, tan print, green print, and blue chambray

Thread to match fabrics

Embroidery floss in these colors: navy blue, brown, green, cream, lavender, light brown, black, light blue, and orange

White quilting thread

1 yard of 44"wide polyester fleece

2 lavender buttons, ½" diameter

7 assorted gray and white buttons, ⅜" diameter

Tracing paper and pencil

Water-soluble marking pen

Appliqué the Designs

Note: Refer to "Needle-Turn Appliqué" on page 6 for general instructions.

1. Trace the patterns individually onto tracing paper and cut apart. Referring to the photo and the color keys, pin the pattern pieces to the desired fabric and cut out, adding a ¼" seam allowance to all edges.

2. Prepare the backgrounds for the blocks according to the individual instructions. Mark the vertical center of each background block.

3. On the spring block, appliqué the shoes ¾" from the bottom edge of the light blue fabric print block, noting their position in relation to the vertical center. Then appliqué the dress, umbrella handle, hand, and sleeve. Appliqué the umbrella, again noting the vertical center.

4. On the summer block, appliqué the curtains on each side of the blue block. Appliqué the lavender banner to the center 1¼" from the top edge. On the green print, mark 1" inside the top and side edges; mark 1¼" inside the bottom edge. Cut on the marked lines. Appliqué the green print border to the block. Appliqué the dress, hands, leaves, and flowers. Appliqué Sue's hat.

5. To complete the summer block, cut the following: 1 light green piece, 1½" x 9"; 1 orange check piece, 2" x 3½"; and 1 yellow piece, 2" x 6½". Sew the orange check and yellow pieces together across one short end, using a ¼" seam (see Diagram 1).

Diagram 1

6. Sew the 9" edge of the light green piece to the right edge of the appliquéd summer block. Then sew the orange check/yellow

piece to the top edge of the appliqué/light green piece (Diagram 2). The finished block will measure 9" x 10".

Diagram 2

7. On the fall block, appliqué the shoes to the orange check block, with the left shoe centered and 1" from the bottom edge. Appliqué the dress, hands and arms, then Sue's hat. Appliqué the orange and dark rust diamonds, referring to the photograph and the pattern for placement.

8. To complete the fall block, cut 1 light green piece, 8½" x 2¼", and 1 light rust piece, 8½" x 2¼". Sew the light green piece to the top of the orange check block; sew the light rust piece to the bottom (see Diagram 3). Appliqué the sun to the light green piece.

Diagram 3

9. On the winter block, appliqué Sue's green print shoes 3¼" from the bottom edge of the block and a scant ¼" right of the vertical center. Appliqué the two blue chambray pieces, the snowman and snowman's hat, then the hand, sleeve, and hat.

Embroider the Details
Note: Refer to "Embroidery Stitches" on page 11 for general instructions.

1. On the spring block, use 2 strands of navy blue floss to backstitch the line parallel to the bottom edge of the umbrella. Sew running stitches for the 2 vertical lines on the umbrella. Make French knots on the sleeve. Using 2 strands of brown floss, stem-stitch the lettering on Sue's dress.

2. On the summer block, use 2 strands of navy blue floss to stem-stitch the lettering on the banner. Buttonhole-stitch around the edge of the green print border, using 2 strands of green floss. Using 2 strands of lavender floss, backstitch the curtain folds, the turquoise flower, and the folds in the banner; satin-stitch the lower folds of the banner. Make a French knot in the center of the turquoise flower. Sew running stitches for the veins in the leaves. Using 3 strands of light blue floss, cross-stitch single stitches on the blue fabric; see the pattern for placement. Using 2 strands of light brown floss, buttonhole-stitch around Sue's hat. Also with light brown floss, sew running stitches in the center of the hat.

3. On the fall block, use 2 strands of navy blue floss to satin-stitch the sun's eyes, and backstitch the eyebrows and nose. Using 2 strands of orange floss, backstitch the eyelids of the sun and the "shine" in its eyes. Using 2 strands of black floss, stem-stitch the lettering. Using 2 strands of light brown floss, sew running stitches around the center of Sue's hat.

4. On the winter block, use 2 strands of light blue floss to stem-stitch the lettering. Using 2 strands of navy blue floss, button-hole-stitch around the center of Sue's hat. Using 1 strand of black floss, backstitch the snowman's mouth. Make French knots for the eyes. Using 2 strands of orange floss, satin-stitch the snowman's nose. Using 3 strands of light brown floss, stem-stitch the snowman's arm.

Assemble the Quilt

1. Sew the assembled summer block to the spring block and sew the fall block to the winter block (Diagram 4). Then sew the top blocks to the bottom blocks without catching the top of the sun in the seam. (You may find that you need to remove the appliqué stitching across the top of the sun, complete the seam, and then appliqué the top of the sun again.)

Diagram 4

2. Satin-stitch the sun's rays, using 2 strands of yellow floss. Sew running stitches ¼" inside and parallel to the outside edge of the sun, using 1 strand of orange floss.

3. Cut 2 border strips from navy blue plaid, each 4" x 20½", for the top and bottom of the quilt and 2 border strips, each 4" x 26½", for the sides.

4. Stitch the left side border strip to the quilt top, aligning the raw edges at the top and stitching to a point 1" from the corner of the quilt top at the bottom. Stitch the top, right side, and bottom borders to the quilt top in that order. Complete the stitching on the left border strip.

5. Center the fleece on the wrong side of the quilt top. Layer the backing, right side up, over the fleece. Baste the 3 layers together, working from the center out. Tun under the raw edges on the sides of the quilt top and fold to the back of the quilt. Slipstitch in place. Repeat along the top and bottom of the quilt.

6. Using white thread, quilt around all design pieces and on one side of every seam joining the blocks. In the spring block, quilt the "wind"; see the pattern. In the summer block, quilt inside the curtains, parallel to the edges. Also quilt vertical parallel lines ⅜" apart in the orange check section. Quilt 2 parallel lines 1" apart on all 4 sides of the border.

7. Sew 2 lavender buttons to the curtains in the summer block. Below the snowman, sew 7 buttons in an arc.

111

Spring

Summer

Button

Button

W

W

w White   Light Brown   Turquoise   Tan

   Lavender   Gold Print   Bright Green   Blue

Winter

W

Buttons

Buttons

Color Key

| | Blue Chambray | | Green Print | | Tan Print | w | White |
| | Blue Print | | Gold Print | | Rose | | |

Color Key

Orange Print Orange Dark Brown Gold

Rust/Black Print Dark Rust Tan

BILL'S
GINGHAM PILLOW

Materials

⅝ yard of 44"-wide tan check fabric
Scraps of cotton fabric in these colors:
blue plaid, blue chambray, brown/black print, tan, and light brown
½ yard of 44"-wide polyester fleece
Thread to match fabrics
Charcoal embroidery floss
14" pillow form
Tracing paper
Chalk
Air-soluble marking pen

Color Key

- Blue Plaid
- Blue Chambray
- Brown/Black Print
- Tan
- Blue-Green
- Light Brown

Appliqué the Design

Note: Refer to "Needle-Turn Appliqué" on page 6 for general instructions.

1. Trace the patterns individually onto tracing paper and cut apart. Referring to the photo and the color keys, pin the pattern pieces to the desired fabric and cut out, adding a ¼" seam allowance to all edges.
2. From the tan check fabric, cut 2 pieces, 17" x 17", for the pillow top and back.
3. Appliqué Bill's shoes, shirt, overalls, hand, sleeve, cuffs, and hat.

Embroider the Details

Note: Refer to "Embroidery Stitches" on page 11 for general instructions.

Using 2 strands of charcoal floss, buttonhole-stitch around the edges of all the pieces, including the internal lines on the cuffs and shoes.

Make the Pillow

1. Cut 2 pieces, 17" x 17", of polyester fleece. Pin fleece pieces to the wrong sides of the tan check pieces.
2. Match the right sides of the tan check pieces. Stitch the outside edges together with a ¼" seam, leaving most of the fourth edge open. Clip the corners. Turn right side out and press lightly.
3. Mark 1½" inside the edges of the pillow cover, allowing for the seam allowance on the open edge. Sew on the marked line, leaving most of the same side open as in the outside edge.
4. Insert the pillow form. Force the pillow back into the pillow cover, pinning ½" inside the marked line to hold the pillow form away from the stitching line. Complete the stitching on the marked line. Slipstitch the opening closed.

SUE'S
GINGHAM PILLOW

Materials

½ yard of 44"-wide lavender check fabric

Scraps of cotton fabric in these colors: purple print, lavendar, tan, yellow/red print, blue/black print, and brown

½ yard of 44"-wide polyester fleece

Thread to match fabrics

Charcoal embroidery floss

14" pillow form

Tracing paper

Chalk

Air-soluble marking pen

Appliqué the Design

Note: Refer to "Needle-Turn Appliqué" on page 6 for general instructions.

1. Trace the patterns individually onto tracing paper and cut apart. Referring to the photo and the color keys, pin the pattern pieces to the desired fabric and cut out, adding a ¼" seam allowance to all edges.

2. From the lavender check fabric, cut 2 pieces, 17" x 17", for the pillow top and back.

3. Appliqué Sue's shoes, skirt, apron, and hand. Appliqué the bodice, sleeve, and hat.

Embroider the Details

Note: Refer to "Embroidery Stitches" on page 11 for general instructions.

Using 2 strands of charcoal floss, buttonhole-stitch around the edges of all pieces, including the internal lines on the shoes and upper sleeve.

Make the Pillow

1. Cut 2 pieces, 17" x 17", of polyester fleece. Pin fleece pieces to the wrong sides of the tan check pieces.

2. Match the right sides of the tan check pieces. Stitch the outside edges together with a ¼" seam, leaving most of the fourth edge open. Clip the corners. Turn right side out and press lightly.

3. Mark 1½" inside the edges of the pillow cover, allowing for the seam allowance on the open edge. Sew on the marked line, leaving most of the same side open as in the outside edge.

4. Insert the pillow form. Force the pillow back into the pillow cover, pinning ½" inside the marked line to hold the pillow form away from the stitching line. Complete the stitching on the marked line. Slipstitch the opening closed.

Color Key

■	Blue/Black Print
▨	Blue Print
□	Lavender
▦	Yellow/Red Print
▤	Tan
■	Brown

About the Authors

With more than thirty-five years of design experience to their credit, Trice Boerens and Terrece Beesley have designed for such companies as Better Homes and Gardens, Oxmoor House, Leisure Arts, The American School of Needlework, *Woman's Day* Magazine, and Coats and Clark.

Trice is well known for her contemporary twists on traditional quiltmaking designs.

She works in numerous artistic mediums, including quilting, watercolor, wood and printmaking. Terrece co-founded the Vanessa-Ann Collection, a leading company in the needlework and craft industry for many years. More than one hundred publications showcase her design talents.

Books from
Martingale & Company

Appliqué
Appliquilt® Your ABCs
Baltimore Bouquets
Basic Quiltmaking Techniques for Hand Appliqué
Coxcomb Quilt
The Easy Art of Appliqué
Folk Art Animals
From a Quilter's Garden
Stars in the Garden
Sunbonnet Sue All Through the Year
Traditional Blocks Meet Appliqué
Welcome to the North Pole

Borders and Bindings
Borders by Design
The Border Workbook
A Fine Finish
Happy Endings
Interlacing Borders
Traditional Quilts with Painless Borders

Design Reference
All New! Copy Art for Quilters
Blockbender Quilts
Color: The Quilter's Guide
Design Essentials: The Quilter's Guide
Design Your Own Quilts
Freedom in Design
The Log Cabin Design Workbook
The Nature of Design
QuiltSkills
Sensational Settings
Surprising Designs from Traditional Quilt Blocks

Foundation/Paper Piecing
Classic Quilts with Precise Foundation Piecing
Crazy but Pieceable
Easy Machine Paper Piecing
Easy Mix & Match Machine Paper Piecing
Easy Paper-Pieced Keepsake Quilts
Easy Paper-Pieced Miniatures
Easy Reversible Vests
Go Wild with Quilts
Go Wild with Quilts—Again!
A Quilter's Ark
Show Me How to Paper Piece

Hand and Machine Quilting/Stitching
Loving Stitches
Machine Needlelace and Other
    Embellishment Techniques
Machine Quilting Made Easy
Machine Quilting with Decorative Threads
Quilting Design Sourcebook
Quilting Makes the Quilt
Thread Magic
Threadplay with Libby Lehman

Home Decorating
Decorate with Quilts & Collections
The Home Decorator's Stamping Book
Living with Little Quilts
Make Room for Quilts
Soft Furnishings for Your Home
Welcome Home: Debbie Mumm

Miniature/Small Quilts
Beyond Charm Quilts
Celebrate! with Little Quilts
Easy Paper-Pieced Miniatures
Fun with Miniature Log Cabin Blocks
Little Quilts All Through the House
Lively Little Logs
Living with Little Quilts
Miniature Baltimore Album Quilts
No Big Deal
A Silk-Ribbon Album
Small Talk

Needle Arts/Ribbonry
Christmas Ribbonry
Crazy Rags
Hand-Stitched Samplers from I Done My Best
Miniature Baltimore Album Quilts
A Passion for Ribbonry
A Silk-Ribbon Album
Victorian Elegance

Quiltmaking Basics
Basic Quiltmaking Techniques for Hand Appliqué
Basic Quiltmaking Techniques for Strip Piecing
The Joy of Quilting
A Perfect Match
Press for Success
The Ultimate Book of Quilt Labels
Your First Quilt Book (or it should be!)

Rotary Cutting/Speed Piecing
Around the Block with Judy Hopkins
All-Star Sampler
Bargello Quilts
Block by Block
Down the Rotary Road with Judy Hopkins
Easy Star Sampler
Magic Base Blocks for Unlimited Quilt Designs
A New Slant on Bargello Quilts
Quilting Up a Storm
Rotary Riot
Rotary Roundup
ScrapMania
Simply Scrappy Quilts
Square Dance
Stripples
Stripples Strikes Again!
Strips that Sizzle
Two-Color Quilts

Seasonal Quilts
Appliquilt® for Christmas
Christmas Ribbonry
Easy Seasonal Wall Quilts
Folded Fabric Fun
Quilted for Christmas
Quilted for Christmas, Book II
Quilted for Christmas, Book III
Quilted for Christmas, Book IV
Welcome to the North Pole

Surface Design/Fabric Manipulation
15 Beads: A Guide to Creating One-of-a-Kind Beads
The Art of Handmade Paper and Collage
Complex Cloth: A Comprehensive Guide
    to Surface Design
Dyes & Paints: A Hands-On Guide to Coloring Fabric
Hand-Dyed Fabric Made Easy

Theme Quilts
The Cat's Meow
Celebrating the Quilt
Class-Act Quilts
The Heirloom Quilt
Honoring the Seasons
Kids Can Quilt
Life in the Country with Country Threads
Lora & Company
Making Memories
More Quilts for Baby
Once Upon a Quilt
Patchwork Pantry
Quick-Sew Celebrations
Quilted Landscapes
Quilted Legends of the West
Quilts: An American Legacy
Quilts for Baby
Quilts from Nature
Through the Window and Beyond

Watercolor Quilts
Awash with Colour
More Strip-Pieced Watercolor Magic
Strip-Pieced Watercolor Magic
Watercolor Impressions
Watercolor Quilts

Wearables
Crazy Rags
Dress Daze
Dressed by the Best
Easy Reversible Vests
More Jazz from Judy Murrah
Quick-Sew Fleece
Sew a Work of Art Inside and Out
Variations in Chenille

Many of these books are available through your local quilt, fabric, craft-supply, or art-supply store. For more information, call, write, fax, or e-mail for our free full-color catalog.

Martingale & Company
PO Box 118
Bothell, WA 98041-0118 USA
1-800-426-3126
International: 1-425-483-3313
24-Hour Fax: 1-425-486-7596
Web site: www.patchwork.com
E-mail: info@patchwork.com

11/98